Dhammapada

WISDOM OF THE BUDDHA

ENGLISH-PĀLI EDITION

Dhammapada

WISDOM OF THE BUDDHA

TRANSLATION BY

Harischandra Kaviratna

THEOSOPHICAL UNIVERSITY PRESS
PASADENA, CALIFORNIA

THEOSOPHICAL UNIVERSITY PRESS
POST OFFICE BOX C
PASADENA, CALIFORNIA 91109–7107
2001

∞

The paper in this book meets the standards for permanence and durability of the Council on Library Resources.

Library of Congress Publication Data

Dhammapada. English & Pali.
Dhammapada: wisdom of the Buddha / translation by Harischandra Kaviratna. — English-Pāli ed. — Pasadena, Calif. : Theosophical University Press, 1980.
xxviii, 177 p. : ill. ; 21 cm.
ISBN 0-911500-39-1 (alk.)
ISBN 0-911500-40-5 pbk (alk. paper)

I. Kaviratna, Harischandra. II. Title.

BQ1372.E54K37 294.3'82—dc19 80-52031
MARC

COVER & FRONTISPIECE: Buddhist stele of gray limestone, 6'7" high, sixth century A.D. *Photograph*: Béla Thinsz; © 1980 by the Museum of Far Eastern Antiquities (Östasiatiska Muséet), Stockholm, Sweden.

Manufactured in the United States of America

CONTENTS

FOREWORD

Buddhist tradition has it that shortly after the passing away of the Lord Buddha five hundred of his Arhats and disciples, led by Kāśyapa, met in council at Rājagaha for the purpose of recalling to mind the truths they had received from their beloved Teacher during the forty-five years of his ministry. Their hope was to implant the salient principles of his message so firmly in memory that they would become a lasting impetus to moral and spiritual conduct, not alone for themselves and the brethren in distant parts of the land, but likewise for all future disciples who would seek to follow in the footsteps of the Awakened One.

With the Teacher no longer among them, the monks found themselves with the responsibility of handing on the teaching and discipline of the Order as faithfully as possible. Having no written texts to rely on, they did as their forebears had before them and prepared their discourses "for recitation," that is, basic themes were repeated with variations in order to impress the ideas on their hearers. At that time, according to the Sinhalese, the *Dhammapada* was orally assembled from the sayings of Gautama given on some three hundred different occasions. Put in verse form the couplets contrast the vanity of hypocrisy, false pride, heedlessness, and selfish desire with the virtues of truthfulness, modesty, vigilance, and self-abnegation. The admonitions are age-old, yet they strike home today, their austerity of purpose fittingly relieved by gentle humor and earthy simile.

Subsequently, several renditions of the *Dhammapada* in the Sanskrit and Chinese languages came into circulation; likewise, a number of stanzas are to be found almost verbatim in other texts of the canonical literature, testifying to the esteem in which its content was anciently held. Since first collated, the *Dhammapada* has become one of the best loved of Buddhist scriptures, recited daily by millions of devotees who chant its verses in Pāli or in their native dialect.

It was inevitable that differences in interpretation of teaching as well as of disciplinary practices would arise, with the result that about a century after the First Council was held a second gathering was called to affirm the purity of the doctrine. It was at this Second Council that the Arhats divided into two main streams, namely, the *Mahāsanghika* or "Great Assembly" and the *Theravāda* or "Doctrine of Elders." These gradually developed into the Mahāyāna or Northern School of Buddhism espoused chiefly in India, Tibet, China, and later Japan, and the Hīnayāna or Southern School whose stronghold is Sri Lanka, Burma, and the countries of Southeast Asia.

The range of Buddhist literature is vast, and much is made of the difference in emphasis between the Mahāyāna and the Hīnayāna: *Mahāyāna* or the "great way or vehicle" is the large "ferryboat" or fuller doctrine of the Lord Buddha that will ferry all beings across the ocean of births and deaths to the "other shore"; *Hīnayāna* or "incomplete or deficient way or vehicle" is, the Mahāyānists say in contempt, the "ferryboat" of inferior quality because it contains less of the vital essence of the Master's wisdom. The Theravādins, the largest branch of Southern Buddhism, repudiate the title, and never refer to themselves as Hīnayānists, because they hold that as the Pāli Canon represents the oldest records of Buddha's life and message they are closer to the source than are the later and more elaborate doctrines of the Mahāyānists. In fact, the Theravādins reverently state that the *Dhammapada* preserves the *buddhavacana* or "word of Buddha." Without doubt it carries the spirit of the Master's teaching, but there is no firm assurance that the Pāli texts represent the most primitive Canon, for there appears to have been more than one collection of scriptures at a very early stage, from which both Pāli and Sanskrit Canons may have developed.

With the passage of years, although both derive inspiration from the same source, the two Schools diverged rather widely. To put it almost too simply, the basic difference lies in this: the goal of the Theravādin is to transmit in utter fidelity the teaching and example of Buddha-Gautama and by the steadfast practice of the virtues to become, in the course of time, an Arhat, one "worthy" of attaining the supreme nirvana or bliss of omniscience; the goal of the Mahāyānist is to become a Bodhisattva, one whose "essence is bodhi or wisdom," and when nirvana is reached to renounce it for the sake of the world and the "weal of gods and men." In this sublime act of compassion is the promise that all beings are potential Buddhas, having the same intrinsic capacity for enlightenment.

Significantly, the same character training and purification

process must be undergone by all devotees, by those who would become Buddha and enter nirvana, and by those who would refuse nirvana, as did Gautama Śākyamuni in the manner of his predecessor Buddhas. But let it not be thought that because the Theravādins do not explicitly delineate the Bodhisattva ideal they lack compassion. In actuality, the power of the Compassionate One is implicit in every word and incident recorded in the Pāli Canon, the *Tripiṭaka* or "Three Baskets," the second of which, namely *Sutta-Piṭaka,* includes the *Dhammapada* and the famed *Jātakamālā* or "stories" that relate the previous "births" of Buddha.

One has only to read a little in this extensive literature to feel the depth of love that filled the Tathāgata. He comes through not as a god or far-off divinity, but as a wonderfully wise and compassionate friend who understands human weakness yet has the gift of inciting the least of us to noble endeavor. His very presence on earth was witness of the "earnest resolve" he had made "a hundred thousand cycles vast and four immensities ago" to join the line of Bodhisattvas who periodically fulfill their *dhamma* of bringing light and hope to a troubled humanity. Were this still not a potent influence in every Buddhist land today the populace would not gather in villages and groves, as they do in Sri Lanka, on full moon nights of their holy days, particularly in the month of Vesak (April/May), to hear once again the monks chanting the sacred verses of how Prince Siddhārtha became Gautama-Bodhisattva out of love for all beings everywhere.

The present translation of the *Dhammapada* by Dr. Harischandra Kaviratna originally appeared as a serial in

Sunrise magazine from August 1970 through September 1971. It has been revised by the translator where needed, and a Glossary of Pāli philosophical terms with Sanskrit equivalents added.

Dr. Kaviratna, a native of Sri Lanka, is equally versed in Sinhalese, Pāli, and Sanskrit, and since youth has been a dedicated researcher into the esoteric implications behind the Vedas, Vedanta, and Buddhist canonical and noncanonical literatures of both Northern and Southern Schools. It is our sincere hope that readers will find food for contemplation in this ancient devotional scripture which for more than twenty centuries has inspired in its hearers a genuine conversion, a "turning about" of the soul from the limitations of the personal toward the light within, the light that is our Self, our refuge, and our strength.

GRACE F. KNOCHE

Pasadena, California
April 15, 1980

INTRODUCTION

BALLADS AND FOLKLORE are the most precious remnants of a glorious and prolific culture that disappeared from the surface of our globe many centuries prior to the dawn of our present civilization. Embedded in age-old legendary poems are the loftiest speculations of our most ancient forebears and, although their culture vanished in the prehistoric past, we may discern its indelible impress upon the extant literature that is the universal heritage of mankind. The *Dhammapada*, the *Bhagavad-Gītā*, and the ascetic poems of the Jains, for instance, perpetuate ethics and norms that were promulgated by the sages of an age that is still shrouded in mystery. Vālmīki and Vyāsa of Āryāvarta, Homer and Pindar of Greece, Druid bard and Mayan priest, Chinese lawgiver and Egyptian hierophant – all echoed these moral values in their epics and systems of thought.

It is evident that even in the earliest dawn of prehistory men used a universal system of signs and symbols to transmit ideas and impressions – without doubt a symbol can more adequately represent a philosophical conception than the written word. Among ancient peoples, such as the Indo-Aryans, literacy and education were not considered of primary importance but merely as aids to interior illumination and religious insight. And indeed, throughout the centuries, mystics of both East and West have attained enlightenment and union with supreme Reality not through scholastic study, not through dialectic discourses, but through self-abnegation and intuitive direct comprehension. Rarely do those of great intellectual stature alone penetrate to the deepest esoteric truths embodied in the symbology of scriptural texts. With this in mind, we can better understand the conviction of the Brahmans that the sacred knowledge would be perverted when put into writing: the Vedas had to be *heard.*

The art of writing, therefore, did not become popular, as the emphasis of education was on the development of memory and its retentive power. If the expounder of a special branch of knowledge wished to protect his system from falling into oblivion, he rendered it into verse, to be sung or chanted; only on rare occasions did he commit it to writing. Paleographic evidence indicates also that writing, in its earliest stages, was used mostly to chronicle historic events; it was not used to impart instruction in mysticism and philosophy, exorcism and religion, for Druid bard and Brahman sage alike considered this a profanation of the esoteric wisdom. In that golden epoch of intuition and memory culture no teacher ever attempted to hand down the sacred knowledge through the medium of script. The immortal epics of poet-philosophers, such as the *Iliad* of Homer and the *Rāmāyana* of Vālmīki, were learned by professional bards and minstrels who recited them in the courts of kings and in the pleasure gardens of the great cities where they drew large cosmopolitan gatherings. They wandered from land to land reciting the traditional ballads in order to entice a zealous following from among the curious. In those days erudition was judged not by a scholar's literary achievements, but by his ability to inspire his hearers to seek wisdom. It was customary also in every court throughout the world for a professional royal minstrel to chant the dynastic history from its beginning up to the time of the living king. For example, in pre-Columbian America, in the palaces of the Incas and Aztecs, reciters were employed who had memorized the genealogy of the solar rulers from the most remote eras.

In this way the hoary wisdom of the Vedas as well as of the non-Vedic literature of India was safely passed from generation to generation by word of mouth for many thousands of years with the utmost preservation of their purity, until in later times they were recorded and printed in book form. Even today in traveling through India, Sri Lanka, or Burma, one may come across numerous individuals who can dictate for days the great works of scripture, grammar, astrology, medicine, and those of other branches of ancient knowledge. Some of this ancient lore is still being orally transmitted, having never been recorded. In Sri Lanka and Burma it is customary for every Buddhist novice to learn the Pāli grammar, lexicons, and the *Dhammapada* by heart. Of course, most of these works are metrical compositions which makes the memorizing of them quite easy. It is rare to find a Buddhist monk in those countries who cannot recite the *Dhammapada* verbatim. It is well known that even the physical philosophers of Miletus and Athens presented their speculations in poetic form. The versification of the *Dhammapada* was done in the Audience Hall of Jeta's Grove at Śrāvasti to enable the followers of Buddha to learn them by rote. Most people think that the versification of these discourses was done after the demise of the Great Master, but my own research leads me to question this.

Although at a certain phase of human culture, learning by rote and oral transmission as a mode of preserving knowledge were admired by the philosophers both in East and West, we cannot underestimate the magnitude of the disadvantages involved. Natural catastrophe, pestilence, war, or other large-scale disasters could destroy the line of priests, bringing to an abrupt end the collective wisdom of untold centuries. This is the exact cause of the disappearance of most of the spoken languages of the archaic past, before the emergence of Sanskrit, Sumerian, Hamitic, and Semitic which, according to our modern philologists, can rightfully claim to be of very early antiquity. How many languages with their literary treasures have vanished from the surface of our planet is still an unsolved question. Dialects which we now know only by name have left us no more than their imprint on the grammatical structures and vocabularies of our modern tongues.

While the age-old method of oral instruction had intrinsic esoteric merit, the ancient philosophers caused neglect of the written word, which did not reemerge before the sixth century B.C. at the dawn of the new intellectual epoch in India. Throughout the Buddhist canon are passages which presuppose the existence of that very ancient religious tradition known as the Vedas, of which the Great Mendicant, Buddha, had acquired mastery under the renowned sage Viśvamitra, "the universal friend." Yet the source of this literature is lost in the mists of time. Although its system of philosophy differs vastly in some of its cardinal tenets from Brahmanism, any critical student is aware that Buddhism contains many of the teachings of the earliest Upanishads. For a fuller understanding of Buddha's spiritual teachings, a regard for the atmosphere in which they developed at the convergence of Vedic and non-Vedic streams is indispensable.

The sacred tradition of the Vedas was already in the possession of the Āryans* many millennia ago. Its mystic religio-philosophy was not only closely related to that of their relatives in Iran (where it took the form of the Avesta), but is also similar to the Eleusinian and Orphic traditions of the Western Āryans who migrated to and established their cultural empires in Greece, Central and Northern Europe, and the Emerald Isle. It should be noted, however, that the seeds of desuetude had been germinating in the Āryan religion before that great family divided.

Orthodox Hindus hold that the Vedas existed even before the creation of the world, coeternal with Brahman. Consequently, most of the hymns of the *Rig-Veda* are not just odes to the beauty of nature, but are musings about a transcendental reality *beyond* visible natural phenomena. It is said that the rishis, while in spiritual trance, came in direct contact with celestial beings of whom they sang, and whom they considered as expressions of the cosmic intelligence, manifestations of the immanent divine principle. Thus they conceived of nature as a living organism controlled by conscious, intelligent entities. To denote these deities, the poets coined a special appellative term, *deva*, for which there is no adequate equivalent in modern European languages. It literally means the "shining one" or the "donor." The rain, therefore, is a deva, because it gives

*This word, as here used for the peoples of Āryāvarta, is derived from the Sanskrit *ārya* (Pāli *ariya*) meaning "noble."

nourishment to all life on earth. Sun, moon, and stars are devas, because they shed light throughout the solar system and universe. The Ganges, Indus, and Sarasvati are deified rivers, because they irrigate the arable lands of Āryāvarta. In addition, many gods of the pluralistic pantheon once were great heroes, warriors, or philanthropists, who later were venerated as devas for their valor or benevolence.

The religion of the Vedas is neither naturalism nor anthropomorphism, neither polytheism nor monotheism, but a unique mysticism, a synthesis of religious streams known to the ancient Āryans. But when esotericism was ousted by exotericism, symbolism by ritualism, idealism by sacerdotalism, this early spiritual vision dwindled into a polytheistic sacrificial creed, and the cultural life of the Āryans became completely dominated by a priesthood. The Brahman priests made every effort to monopolize for themselves the religious hymns of the Vedas and the ballads which the Āryans sang in praise of the deified natural forces, thus arrogating to themselves as much power as possible. Dr. T. W. Rhys Davids writes in *Buddhist India:*

> We cannot, therefore, be far wrong if we suppose they [the Brahmans] were not merely indifferent to the use of writing as a means of handing on the books so lucrative to themselves, but were even strongly opposed to a method so dangerous to their exclusive privileges. And we ought not to be surprised to find that the oldest manuscripts on bark or palm leaf known in India are Buddhist; that the earliest written records on stone and metal are Buddhist; that it is the Buddhists who first made use of writing to record their canonical books; . . . —p. 119

And so it was that with the advent of the Buddha the art

of writing was given renewed impetus, and began to rise again from the gloomy limbo where it had been concealed for so long by the Brahman priesthood.

For a genealogy of Prince Siddhārtha Gautama Śākya Muni, full-blown lotus of the solar dynasty, Lion of the Śākya clan, prince and heir-apparent of the city state of Kapilavastu, we have to rely mostly on the literary material embedded in the immortal Sanskrit poetical works of Aśvaghosha and Kshemendra. Aśvaghosha flourished in the second century A.D. at the court of the Kushan King Kanishka in Northern India and recorded the Buddhist chronicles which had been handed down through oral tradition. Kshemendra, a great Buddhist poet of Kashmir in the eleventh century, wrote a poetical chronology of the dynastic history of the Śākya clan in his *Avadāna Kalpalatā,* an epic work which was translated into Tibetan in 1272 A.D. by Sovi-rton Lochava under the supervision of Phags-pa, spiritual instructor of Kublai Khan. The original Sanskrit text was lost for many centuries but recovered in 1882 by the Buddhist scholar Sri S. C. Das in the Tibetan printing establishment at Potala. The *Śākya-utpatti* ("Birth of the Śākya clan") of Kshemendra, as well as Pāli commentaries and Tibetan legends, together give a comprehensive account of the origin of the Śākya clan.

Almost thirty miles to the south of the foothills of the Himalayas, a rolling plain extends for hundreds of miles along the Nepalese frontier, verdant and picturesque, rich in scenic delights and silent forest glades through which flow sparkling streams. In this ideal retreat Buddhist tradition has it that a bodhisattva, Kapila Gautama Muni, lived about three centuries before the advent of Gautama Buddha.

Sometime between 950 and 900 B.C. there reigned a mighty king named Virudhaka, lord of a vast confederation of vassal states, and descendant of the Ikshvāku dynasty. On a pleasure trip he beheld a most charming young princess and felt himself compelled to make her a matrimonial proposal, which the princess accepted only on condition that the king appoint her youngest son, instead of her eldest, to be his heir to the throne of Kośala. In due time the queen reminded her lord of the promise he had made; the king was distressed by the demand that he break the Vedic convention, but the four older sons volunteered to accept banishment. They loaded their chariots and rode towards the Himalayas whose snow-covered peaks glittered on the far horizon. After some days they reached the monastery of the celebrated sage Kapila Gautama.

The princes were well received and, instructed by the sage, they founded a flourishing metropolis which became known as Kapilavastu. After many centuries of benign rule, the sovereignty of the Śākya kingdom fell to King Sinhahanu. During his reign Kapilavastu became a center of international trade, learning, and spiritual culture.* King Sinhahanu had four sons and four daughters. The oldest son was Prince Śuddhodana. He became known as King of Law, for he governed in accordance with the rules pre-

*The precise location of this city is not firmly established, though excavations in 1971 at Piprahwa, in the northeastern corner of the Basti district on the Nepalese frontier, uncovered a monastery constructed in four stages. Also at Piprahwa is a stupa erected in the time of King Aśoka (273-232 B.C.), which bears an inscription suggesting that relics found therein are those of members of the Śākya family, close relatives of Gautama Buddha, possibly including those of Buddha himself.

scribed by Manu for righteous kings, and was loved by all his subjects.

King Śuddhodana married his cousin Māyā and, after her death, another cousin, Mahā-Prajāpatī. Queen Māyā was the personification of beauty and purity, compassion, cosmic love, and intelligence. In esoteric schools she was considered the materialization of a divine vision: Queen Māyā had all the virtues to become the mother of the universal Lord of Compassion, and yet after several years of married life the royal couple had not been blessed with a child. The account of the annunciation of the Śākya prince who was to become Buddha, known to every Buddhist in Sanskrit, Pāli, or his native vernacular, is charmingly rendered into English by Sir Edwin Arnold, one of the great poets of the nineteenth century who spent a large part of his life in India. His classic, *The Light of Asia,* relates:

> That night the wife of King Suddhōdana,
> Maya the Queen, asleep beside her Lord,
> Dreamed a strange dream; dreamed that a star from
> heaven –
> Splendid, six-rayed, in color rosy-pearl,
> Whereof the token was an Elephant
> Six-tusked, and white as milk of Kamadhuk –
> Shot through the void; and, shining into her,
> Entered her womb upon the right. Awaked,
> Bliss beyond mortal mother's filled her breast,
> And over half the earth a lovely light
> Forewent the morn. The strong hills shook; the waves
> Sank lulled; all flowers that blow by day came forth
> As 'twere high noon; down to the farthest hells
> Passed the Queen's joy, as when warm sunshine thrills
> Wood-glooms to gold, and into all the deeps

A tender whisper pierced. "Oh ye," it said,
"The dead that are to live, the live who die,
Uprise, and hear, and hope! Buddha is come!"
Whereat in Limbos numberless much peace
Spread, and the world's heart throbbed, and a wind blew
With unknown freshness over lands and seas.
And when the morning dawned, and this was told,
The grey dream-readers said "The dream is good!
The Crab is in conjunction with the Sun;
The Queen shall bear a boy, a holy child
Of wondrous wisdom, profiting all flesh,
Who shall deliver men from ignorance,
Or rule the world, if he will deign to rule."

In this wise was the holy Buddha born.

It was the age-old custom that the first confinement of a young mother should take place in the home of her parents, so, when Queen Māyā felt that the blessed day was drawing near, she intimated her desire to go to her childhood home for the great event which the whole world was anticipating. The Lord of Kapilavastu caused the road connecting the two cities of the Śākyas to be swept and decorated, embellished with festoons and garlands. It was the month of flowers; the day was Vaisākha (Vesak) Full Moon Day in the year 623 B.C.* Between the two cities lay the famous pleasure garden Lumbinī, and it was here, as the cortège paused on the journey, that the holy child saw the

*The dates of Śākyamuni's birth, death, and parinirvana have been variously calculated. Buddhist scholars have used at least three different calendars to compute these dates, as well as various astrological configurations. In addition, Western scholars have employed their own calendric ways of reckoning. With such diversity of opinions, no exact date can be determined.

light of day among blossoming trees and warbling birds, while strains of heavenly music filled the air and soft breezes enriched with a celestial aroma blew throughout the Śākya kingdom.

Buddhist tradition records that as soon as Prince Siddhārtha was born, King Śuddhodana summoned the most erudite scholars and astrologers to the palace of Kapilavastu to cast the horoscope of the newborn babe. After examining the planetary positions, seven of the eight astrologers announced that the prince would become either the universal monarch of the present cycle, or he would retire from the world and become Buddha. Kaundañña alone, youngest member of the Astrological Council, predicted that Siddhārtha would indeed abdicate the throne of the Śākyas and become omniscient Buddha to save suffering humanity. Later, when the prince renounced the throne, Kaundañña also gave up the "householder life" and joined a small group of contemplatives in the forest. It was this community of five ascetics with whom Gautama-Siddhārtha spent six years practicing austerities so severe that, when near death, he perceived that enlightenment was not to be attained by this means. It was then he adopted the system of moderation that came to be known as the Middle Way. After Gautama's illumination under the Bodhi tree, these five monks became his earliest disciples.

Another who correctly foresaw the infant's destiny was the venerable sage Asita (or Kāla Devala), who was spiritual guide and mentor to King Śuddhodana and to his father before him. On learning of the birth of Siddhārtha, the sage hastened to the palace and, observing the distinguishing marks on the child, the aged Asita wept — not for the prince, but for himself, as his great age would prevent him from seeing the child grow up to become Buddha.

As King Śuddhodana strongly believed in the prediction that his son would be a world monarch, he had him instructed by Viśvamitra in the extensive curriculum befitting such a prince, including the Vedas and all systems of mysticism then current. It is noteworthy that the young man was taught to decipher pictographs as well as the sign language of cave dwellers and those plying the seas. In fact, from the vivid descriptions in ancient Sanskrit and Tibetan Buddhist works, and even from those in the rival literatures of the Jains and Vedantins, we may safely deduce that the Buddha had mastered all the sciences, arts, and languages known in India at that time.

We have here an interesting parallel between King Śuddhodana of Kapilavastu appointing the sage Viśvamitra as teacher to Prince Siddhārtha and the selection by King Philip of Macedonia of the great philosopher Aristotle to be preceptor to Prince Alexander. In both Āryan princes the age-old dream of establishing an invincible brotherhood of peoples was ingrained in their racial soul; but while Alexander spent most of his short life in military expeditions in an effort to expand the borders of his empire, Prince Siddhārtha bade adieu to a worldly realm in order to establish an imperishable, eternal kingdom of the spirit.

The seventh-sixth centuries B.C. marked a new historical epoch in the religious evolution of Northern India. The racial intellect of the time was compelled to face two opposing psychological trends. The solution lay in the emergence of a magnetic individual who could successfully synthesize the realism of the physical philosophers with the idealism of the ancient Vedas, one who could blend the best of the old with the vigorous and constructive elements of the new. This mighty task, undertaken by Gautama Śākyamuni, was successfully accomplished by setting the "Wheel of the Sacred Law in motion" – that eternal Law which is forever valid, for the past, the present, and for eternities to come. This Law is preserved for posterity in the *Dhammapada*, a sublime ethical treatise of twenty-six cantos, which is to millions of Buddhists what the *Bhagavad-Gītā* is to Hindus. Although it is not known when it was first committed to writing, its content suggests a direct descent from spiritual instruction given by Gautama Buddha. Extensive research confirms that these teachings express a universal wisdom, a rediscovery of the eternal Buddha Dharma which could rightly be termed the Sanātana Dharma or "eternal wisdom."

Dhammapada – the path of *dhamma* (Sanskrit *dharma*, a word comprising the essential ideas contained in the words truth, virtue, and law) – was compiled at the First Council of Buddhist Elders three weeks after the Master's passing. It is therefore the oldest anthology on Buddhism extant. The work consists of a systematic collection of stanzas, terse yet elegant, giving the quintessence of Buddhist wisdom. These stanzas were the distillation of various sermons delivered by Buddha to kings and queens, to ministers and merchants, cowherds and peasants, to grieving mothers, distressed lovers, monks, paupers, saints, and criminals. The first verse of the *Dhammapada* is a direct attack on the dialectical materialism prevalent at the time of Buddha. Mind is not a by-product of physical elements; according to Buddha, mind precedes everything that exists. Nor is the destruction of the physical body the end of human existence. The external cosmos is a creation of mind integrated into a cosmic order of cause and effect.

The Master admonished his leading Arhats not to compel his followers to learn Ardha-Māgadhī in order to understand his doctrine. Therefore, when Buddhism expanded, as it rapidly did, beyond the frontiers of Āryāvarta, the missionaries began to translate the Dharma into numerous dialects and vernaculars. We know, for example, that *Dharmapadaṃ,* an early Prakrit treatise, was composed during the fourth century B.C., and that about a century later, the first Buddhist king, Aśoka, sent his son, Arhat Mahinda, to Sri Lanka, where he and his disciples made the first Sinhalese version of this ethical manual, titled *Dhampiyā.* Unfortunately, this earliest rendition of *Dhammapada* in Sinhalese-Prakrit fell into oblivion soon after Buddhist prelates retranslated it into Pāli along with the other works of the *Tripiṭaka* in 88-76 B.C.

It may be noted that Pāli, like most European languages, has no alphabet of its own; in Sri Lanka it was written in Sinhalese script, while Burmese Buddhists used their own characters to write the Pāli text. The language used by Buddha, Ardha-Māgadhī dialect, is very similar to the literary language of the Jains. Pāli has the coloring of this dialect. Because in a living language terms undergo continual modification as the thought life of the nation changes, the Theravāda scholars tried to retranslate the Buddha Dhamma from Sinhalese back into Pāli, which has the Sinhalese idiom unaltered with very little Sanskrit influence upon it. Most of the Indian versions are no longer extant, either in printed or manuscript form, in any of the museum libraries of the world. Only a few birchbark manuscripts in Prakrit were discovered in the early part of the nineteenth century in northwestern India.

A Chinese *Dhammapada,* translated from the Sanskrit, was not lost; it was the first book, along with the rest of the *Tripiṭaka,* ever to be produced in a printing press and was made from wooden blocks in 972 A.D. But not until 1885 was the Pāli *Dhammapada,* which had been lost to India for twenty-two centuries or so, reintroduced into that country in Devanāgarī transliteration by my paternal uncle, Ven. B. Sri Dharmapala Nayaka Thero of Batapola, under the guidance of Rt. Ven. C. A. Sīlakkandha Nayaka Thero of Dodanduwa, Sri Lanka.

Thirty years earlier, in 1855, a young Danish scholar, Victor Fausbøll, published the first European edition of the *Dhammapada* in a Latin translation, with Pāli text, and selections of native commentary. Subsequent renditions in German, English, and French followed, making the scripture more readily available to Western students. Later, Dr. E. W. Burlingame's three-volume translation of the voluminous commentary on the *Dhammapada,* written by the renowned Indian scholar Buddhaghosha in the early part of the fifth century A.D., provided the modern reader with a wealth of legendary and historic details regarding the various episodes and circumstances which led to the utterance of these verses. Were Buddha to come to the world today, however, he would probably not countenance some of the stories that accompany his ethical teachings. For instance, he did not totally deny the existence of spirit in his *anātman* (Pāli *anattā*) doctrine, but used negative terms to illustrate and clarify the state of spirit.

The volumes on the *Dhammapada* in my possession are

mostly in the Devanāgarī and Sinhalese scripts, the Pāli text of which has undergone very little distortion, although the commentaries and translations differ greatly. Some commentators have curious and artificial renderings, which are not akin to the streams of Buddhist and Vedic thought prevalent in India during the time of Buddha. Most of the European and Indian translators have based their renditions upon these artificial commentaries without any deep penetration into the philosophic currents of that early period.

For this present small volume, I have diligently compared the best European translations of the *Dhammapada* with Sanskrit, Burmese, and Chinese versions. Special care has been taken to bring out a faithful word-for-word rendition that is lucid, free of bias and, as far as possible, true to the wisdom and pristine grace of the original Pāli texts.

– DR. HARISCHANDRA KAVIRATNA

27 February 1980
Oriental Institute
Batapola, Sri Lanka

ACKNOWLEDGMENTS

ACKNOWLEDGMENT is hereby made to *Sunrise* magazine for permission to publish this translation in book form; to the editorial and printing staffs of Theosophical University Press for their untiring labors during the preparation of the manuscript and through every stage of publication. I have a deep sense of gratitude to the late James A. Long, Leader of the Theosophical Society, Pasadena, California who, prior to his death, inspired me to embark upon this rendition. I am also indebted to his successor in office, Grace F. Knoche, for many valuable suggestions.

Grateful thanks are extended to the Rt. Ven. G. Puññasāra Maha Thero, Spiritual Instructor at the Government Central College of Madamba, Sri Lanka; also to K. D. Paranavitana, Assistant Archivist, Department of National Archives, Colombo, for supplying the photograph of the wooden covers and first and last pages of the palm leaf manuscript of the *Dhammapada* which is considered the oldest extant copy of the scripture in the National Archives of Sri Lanka.

Lastly, a special word of appreciation to my beloved wife for her unfailing support and to my daughter Savitri who did the several typings required for the entire manuscript in Pāli and English.

H. K.

PALM LEAF MANUSCRIPT

(*Overleaf*)

Outer wooden covers ("Kambā") and the first and last pages of the Pāli text of the *Dhammapada* in Sinhalese characters. This palm leaf manuscript (17½" x 2½") is believed to be the oldest extant copy of the scripture.

The upper cover depicts the Bodhi tree in green, under which the mendicant Gautama is said to have attained supreme enlightenment, and eight stupas colored amber against a red background. The lower cover shows a relic casket and two stupas beside the Sri Pada Mountain with the Buddha's footprint, and portrays also the Great Passing of the Buddha into Parinirvana.

Photo: Courtesy of K. D. Paranavitana, Assistant Archivist, Department of National Archives, Colombo, Sri Lanka.

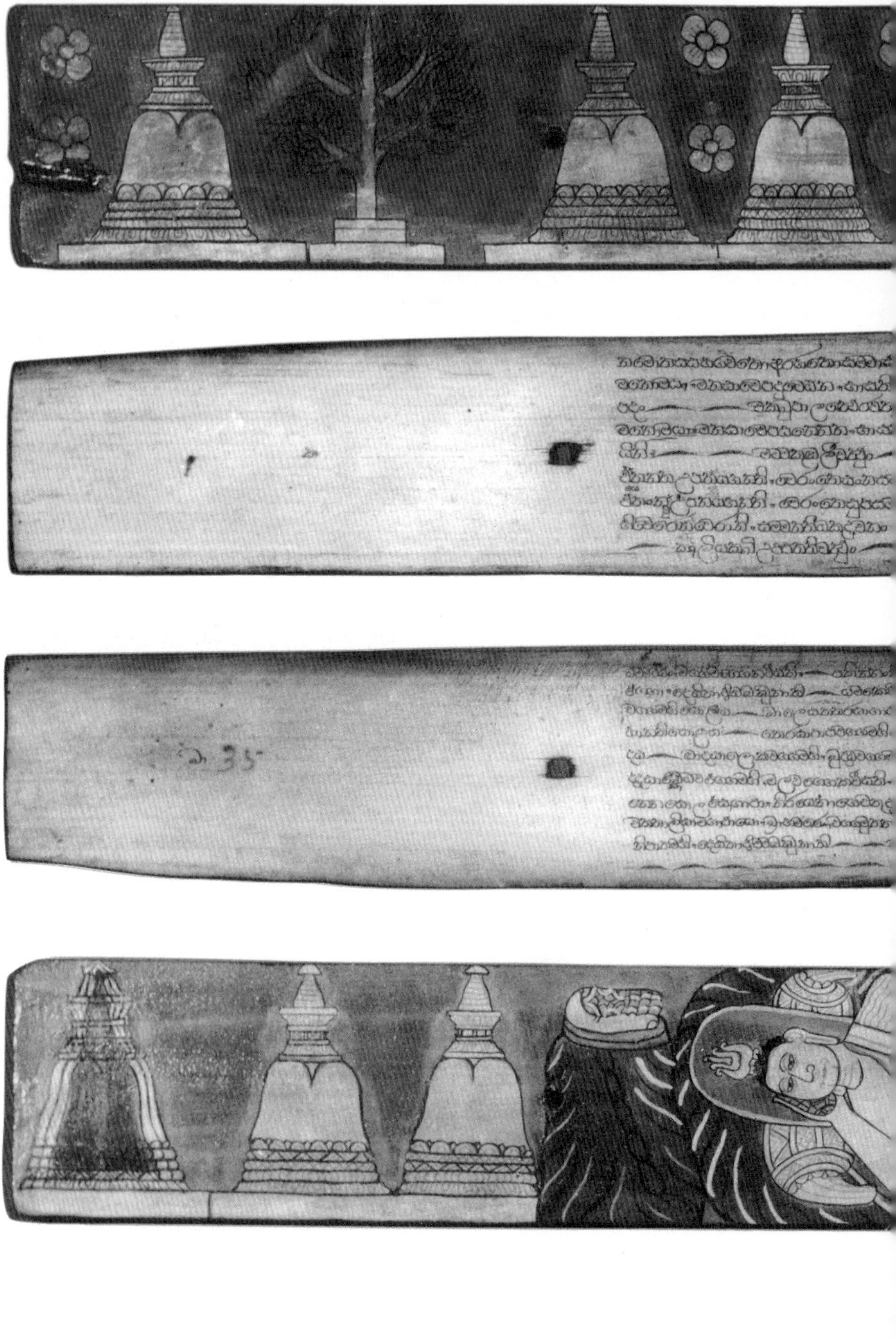

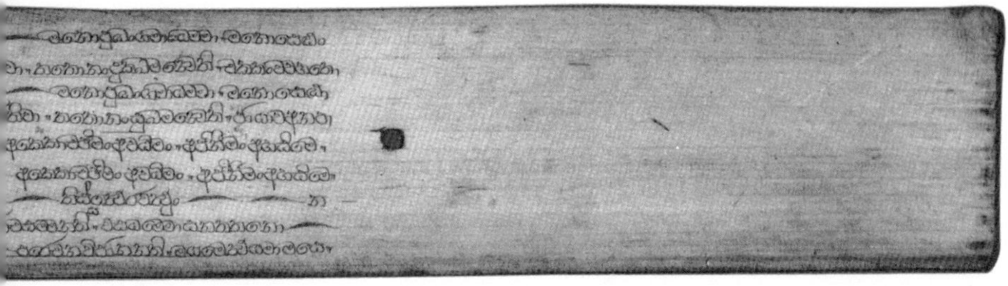

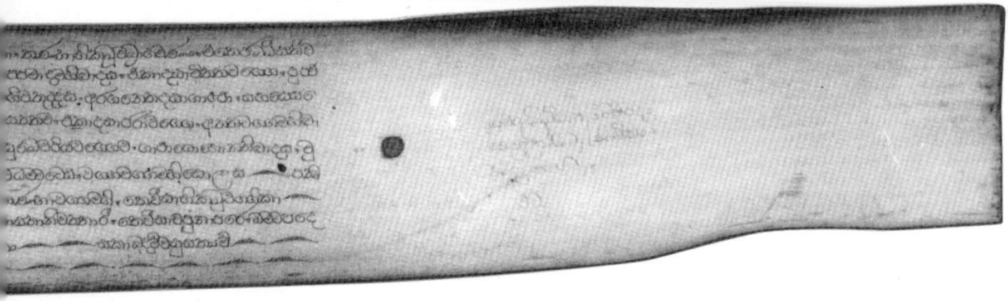

Dhammapada

WISDOM OF THE BUDDHA

DHAMMAPADAṂ

namo tassa bhagavato arahato sammāsambuddhassa

THE PATH OF TRUTH

Salutations to the Blessed One, the
Exalted One, the Fully Enlightened One!

YAMAKAVAGGO PAṬHAMO

1

manopubbaṅgamā dhammā manoseṭṭhā manomayā
manasā ce paduṭṭhena bhāsati vā karoti vā
tato naṃ dukkhamanveti cakkaṃ'va vahato padaṃ

2

manopubbaṅgamā dhammā manoseṭṭhā manomayā
manasā ce pasannena bhāsati vā karoti vā
tato naṃ sukhamanveti chāyā'va anapāyinī

3

akkocchi maṃ avadhi maṃ ajini maṃ ahāsi me
ye taṃ upanayhanti veraṃ tesaṃ na sammati

4

akkocchi maṃ avadhi maṃ ajini maṃ ahāsi me
ye taṃ na upanayhanti veraṃ tesûpasammati

5

na hi verena verāni sammantîdha kudācanaṃ
averena ca sammanti esa dhammo sanantano

The Twin Verses – CANTO I

1

All the phenomena of existence have mind as their precursor, mind as their supreme leader, and of mind are they made. If with an impure mind one speaks or acts, suffering follows him in the same way as the wheel follows the foot of the drawer (of the chariot).

2

All the phenomena of existence have mind as their precursor, mind as their supreme leader, and of mind are they made. If with a pure mind one speaks or acts, happiness follows him like his shadow that never leaves him.

3

The hatred of those who harbor such ill feelings as, "He reviled me, assaulted me, vanquished me and robbed me," is never appeased.

4

The hatred of those who do not harbor such ill feelings as, "He reviled me, assaulted me, vanquished me and robbed me," is easily pacified.

5

Through hatred, hatreds are never appeased; through non-hatred are hatreds always appeased — and this is a law eternal.

6

pare ca na vijānanti mayamettha yamāmase
ye ca tattha vijānanti tato sammanti medhagā

7

subhānupassiṃ viharantaṃ indriyesu asaṃvutaṃ
bhojanamhi amattaññuṃ kusītaṃ hīnavīriyaṃ
taṃ ve pasahati māro vāto rukkhaṃ'va dubbalaṃ

8

asubhānupassiṃ viharantaṃ indriyesu susaṃvutaṃ
bhojanamhi ca mattaññuṃ saddhaṃ āraddhavīriyaṃ
taṃ ve nappasahati māro vāto selaṃ'va pabbataṃ

9

anikkasāvo kāsāvaṃ yo vatthaṃ paridahessati
apeto damasaccena na so kāsāvamarahati

10

yo ca vantakasāv'assa sīlesu susamāhito
upeto damasaccena sa ve kāsāvamarahati

11

asāre sāramatino sāre cā'sāradassino
te sāraṃ nâdhigacchanti micchāsaṅkappagocarā

6

Most people never realize that all of us here shall one day perish. But those who do realize that truth settle their quarrels peacefully.

7

The pleasure-seeker who finds delight in physical objects, whose senses are unsubdued, who is immoderate in eating, indolent and listless, him Māra (the Evil One) prevails against, as does the monsoon wind against a weak-rooted tree.

8

He who perceives no pleasure in physical objects, who has perfect control of his senses, is moderate in eating, who is unflinching in faith, energetic, him Māra does not prevail against any more than does the wind against a rocky mountain.

9

He who dons the yellow robe without even cleansing himself of sensuality, who is devoid of self-restraint and truthfulness, is indeed not fit for the yellow robe.

10

He who is purged of all sensuality, firmly established in moral virtues, possessed of self-restraint and truthfulness, is indeed fit for the yellow robe.

11

Those who take the non-real for the real and the real for the non-real and thus fall victims to erroneous notions, never reach the essence of reality.

12

sāraññ ca sārato ñatvā asāraññ ca asārato
te sāraṃ adhigacchanti sammāsaṅkappagocarā

13

yathā agāraṃ ducchannaṃ vuṭṭhi samativijjhati
evaṃ abhāvitaṃ cittaṃ rāgo samativijjhati

14

yathā agāraṃ succhannaṃ vuṭṭhi na samativijjhati
evaṃ subhāvitaṃ cittaṃ rāgo na samativijjhati

15

idha socati pecca socati pāpakārī ubhayattha socati
so socati so vihaññati disvā kammakiliṭṭhamattano

16

idha modati pecca modati katapuñño ubhayattha modati
so modati so pamodati disvā kammavisuddhimattano

17

idha tappati pecca tappati pāpakārī ubhayattha tappati
pāpaṃ me kataṃ ti tappati bhiyyo tappati duggatiṃ gato

18

idha nandati pecca nandati katapuñño ubhayattha nandati
puññaṃ me kataṃ ti nandati bhiyyo nandati suggatiṃ gato

12

Having realized the essential as the essential and the nonessential as the nonessential, they by thus following correct thinking attain the essential.

13

As the monsoon rain pierces through the roof of an ill-thatched house, so lust enters the undisciplined mind.

14

As the monsoon rain does not enter a well-thatched house, so lust does not enter a well-disciplined mind.

15

The sinner laments here, laments hereafter, and he laments in both worlds. Having seen himself sullied by his sinful deeds, the evildoer grieves and is afflicted.

16

The doer of wholesome deeds rejoices here and rejoices hereafter; thus he rejoices in both places. Having beheld his pure deeds he rejoices exceedingly.

17

He repents here, repents hereafter, the evildoer repents in both worlds. "Evil has been committed by me," thinking thus he repents. Having taken the path of evil he repents even more.

18

He rejoices here, he rejoices hereafter, the doer of wholesome deeds rejoices in both worlds. "Good has been committed by me," thinking thus he rejoices. Having taken the celestial path, he rejoices exceedingly.

19

bahumpi ce sahitaṃ bhāsamāno
na takkaro hoti naro pamatto
gopo'va gāvo gaṇayaṃ paresaṃ
na bhāgavā sāmaññassa hoti

20

appampi ce sahitaṃ bhāsamāno
dhammassa hoti anudhammacārī
rāgañ ca dosañ ca pahāya mohaṃ
sammappajāno suvimuttacitto
anupādiyāno idha vā huraṃ vā
sa bhāgavā sāmaññassa hoti

19

A heedless man, though he utters much of the Canon, but does not act accordingly, is like unto a cowherd who counts the cattle of others. He is, verily, not a sharer of the fruit of the monastic life.

20

A man, though he recites only a little of the Canon, but acts according to the precepts of the Sacred Law, who, having got rid of lust, hatred and delusion, has firmly established himself in liberated thought, and clinging to no worldly possessions here or hereafter – such a one becomes indeed a sharer of the true fruit of the monastic life.

APPAMĀDAVAGGO DUTIYO

21

appamādo amatapadaṃ pamādo maccuno padaṃ
appamattā na mīyanti ye pamattā yathā matā

22

etaṃ visesato ñatvā appamādamhi paṇḍitā
appamāde pamodanti ariyānaṃ gocare ratā

23

te jhāyino sātatikā niccaṃ daḷhaparakkamā
phusanti dhīrā nibbānaṃ yogakkhemaṃ anuttaraṃ

24

uṭṭhānavato satīmato sucikammassa nisammakārino
saññatassa ca dhammajīvino appamattassa yaso'bhivaḍḍhati

25

uṭṭhānen'appamādena saṃyamena damena ca
dīpaṃ kayirātha medhāvī yaṃ ogho nâbhikīrati

26

pamādamanuyuñjanti bālā dummedhino janā
appamādañ ca medhāvī dhanaṃ seṭṭhaṃ'va rakkhati

On Vigilance – Canto II

21

Vigilance is the path to immortality; non-vigilance is the path to death; the vigilant do not die; the non-vigilant, though alive, are like unto the dead.

22

Knowing this outstanding feature of vigilance, the wise delight in vigilance, rejoicing in the ways of the Noble Ones (*ariya*).

23

Those wise ones, contemplative, ever-striving sages of great prowess, realize nirvana, the incomparable bliss of yoga (union).

24

Greatly increasing is the glory of him who exerts himself, is thoughtful, pure in character, analytical, self-restrained, vigilant, and lives according to Dhamma (the Law).

25

Through diligence, vigilance, self-restraint and subjugation of the senses, the wise aspirant makes an island for himself that no flood could engulf.

26

Thoughtless men of great ignorance sink into negligence. But the wise man guards vigilance as his supreme treasure.

27

mā pamādamanuyuñjetha mā kāmaratisanthavaṃ
appamatto hi jhāyanto pappoti vipulaṃ sukhaṃ

28

pamādamappamādena yadā nudati paṇḍito
paññāpāsādamāruyha asoko sokiniṃ pajaṃ
pabbataṭṭho'va bhummaṭṭhe dhīro bāle avekkhati

29

appamatto pamattesu suttesu bahujāgaro
abalassaṃ'va sīghasso hitvā yāti sumedhaso

30

appamādena maghavā devānaṃ seṭṭhataṃ gato
appamādaṃ pasaṃsanti pamādo garahito sadā

31

appamādarato bhikkhu pamāde bhayadassi vā
saṃyojanaṃ aṇuṃ thūlaṃ ḍahaṃ aggī'va gacchati

32

appamādarato bhikkhu pamāde bhayadassi vā
abhabbo parihānāya nibbānass'eva santike

27

Betake yourselves not unto negligence; do not indulge in sensuous pleasures. For the vigilant and thoughtful aspirant acquires an amplitude of bliss.

28

When the wise man casts off laxity through vigilance, he is like unto a man who, having ascended the high tower of wisdom, looks upon the sorrowing people with an afflicted heart. He beholds suffering ignorant men as a mountaineer beholds people in a valley.

29

Vigilant among the heedless, wakeful among the sleeping ones, the wise man forges ahead, as a swift steed outstrips a horse of lesser strength.

30

Through vigilance, did Maghavān (Indra) attain to the sovereignty of the gods. Vigilance is ever praised and negligence is ever loathed by the sages.

31

The bhikkhu (monk) who delights in vigilance, who regards negligence with abhorrence, advances, consuming all subtle and gross fetters, like the fire.

32

The bhikkhu who delights in vigilance, who looks upon negligence with abhorrence, is not liable to fall back, because he is indeed close to nirvana.

CITTAVAGGO TATIYO

33

phandanaṃ capalaṃ cittaṃ dūrakkhaṃ dunnivārayaṃ
ujuṃ karoti medhāvī usukāro'va tejanaṃ

34

vārijo'va thale khitto okamokata ubbhato
pariphandati'daṃ cittaṃ māradheyyaṃ pahātave

35

dunniggahassa lahuno yattha kāmanipātino
cittassa damatho sādhu cittaṃ dantaṃ sukhâvahaṃ

36

sududdasaṃ sunipuṇaṃ yattha kāmanipātinaṃ
cittaṃ rakkhetha medhāvī cittaṃ guttaṃ sukhâvahaṃ

37

dūraṅgamaṃ ekacaraṃ asarīraṃ guhâsayaṃ
ye cittaṃ saṃyamessanti mokkhanti mārabandhanā

The Mind – Canto III

33

The discerning man straightens his mind, which is fickle and unsteady, difficult to guard and restrain, as the skilled fletcher straightens the shaft (of the arrow).

34

As the fish, taken out of its watery home and thrown on land, thrashes around, so does the mind tremble, while freeing itself from the dominion of Māra (the Evil One).

35

The mind is unstable and flighty. It wanders wherever it desires. Therefore it is good to control the mind. A disciplined mind brings happiness.

36

The mind is incomprehensible and exceedingly subtle. It wanders wherever it desires. Therefore, let the wise aspirant watch over the mind. A well-guarded mind brings happiness.

37

Those who control the mind which wanders afar, solitary, incorporeal, and which resides in the inner cavern (of the heart), will liberate themselves from the shackles of Māra.

38

anavaṭṭhitacittassa saddhammaṃ avijānato
pariplavapasādassa paññā na paripūrati

39

anavassutacittassa ananvāhatacetaso
puññapāpapahīnassa n'atthi jāgarato bhayaṃ

40

kumbhūpamaṃ kāyam imaṃ viditvā
nagarūpamaṃ cittam idaṃ ṭhapetvā
yodhetha māraṃ paññāyudhena
jitañ ca rakkhe anivesano siyā

41

aciraṃ vat'ayaṃ kāyo paṭhaviṃ adhisessati
chuddho apetaviññāṇo niratthaṃ'va kaḷiṅgaraṃ

42

diso disaṃ yaṃ taṃ kayirā verī vā pana verinaṃ
micchāpaṇihitaṃ cittaṃ pāpiyo naṃ tato kare

43

na taṃ mātā pitā kayirā aññe vā'pi ca ñātakā
sammāpaṇihitaṃ cittaṃ seyyaso naṃ tato kare

38

He whose mind is not steady, who is ignorant of the true Dhamma, whose tranquillity is ruffled, the wisdom of such a man does not come to fullness.

39

Fear has he none, whose mind is not defiled by passion, whose heart is devoid of hatred, who has surpassed (the dichotomy of) good and evil and who is vigilant.

40

Knowing the corporeal body to be fragile, as an earthen jar, and fortifying the mind like a citadel, let the wise man fight Māra with the sword of wisdom. He should now protect what he has won, without attachment.

41

Alas! ere long, this corporeal body will lie flat upon the earth, unheeded, devoid of consciousness, like a useless log of wood.

42

An ill-directed mind does greater harm to the self than a hater does to another hater or an enemy to another enemy.

43

Neither father nor mother, nor any other kindred, can confer greater benefit than does the well-directed mind.

PUPPHAVAGGO CATUTTHO

44

ko imaṃ paṭhaviṃ vijessati yamalokañ ca imaṃ sadevakaṃ
ko dhammapadaṃ sudesitaṃ kusalo puppham iva pacessati

45

sekho paṭhaviṃ vijessati yamalokañ ca imaṃ sadevakaṃ
sekho dhammapadaṃ sudesitaṃ kusalo puppham iva pacessati

46

pheṇūpamaṃ kāyam imaṃ viditvā
marīcidhammaṃ abhisambudhāno
chetvāna mārassa papupphakāni
adassanaṃ maccurājassa gacche

47

pupphāni h'eva pacinantaṃ byāsattamanasaṃ naraṃ
suttaṃ gāmaṃ mahogho'va maccu ādāya gacchati

The Flowers — Canto IV

44

Who shall gain victory over this earth together with the domain of Yama (ruler of the Underworld) with its gods? Who shall find the well-proclaimed Dhammapada (path of truth), even as the expert gardener selects the choicest flower?

45

The disciple will gain victory over the earth and the realm of Yama together with its gods. The true disciple will indeed find the well-proclaimed Dhammapada, even as the expert gardener selects the choicest flower.

46

Recognizing this corporeal body to be evanescent as foam, comprehending this worldly nature as a mirage, and having broken the flower-arrows of Cupid (Māra), the true aspirant will go beyond the realm of the Evil One.

47

The hedonist who seeks only the blossoms of sensual delights, who indulges only in such pleasures, him the Evil One carries off, as a flood carries off the inhabitants of a sleeping village.

48

pupphāni h'eva pacinantaṃ byāsattamanasaṃ naraṃ
atittam y'eva kāmesu antako kurute vasaṃ

49

yathā'pi bhamaro pupphaṃ vaṇṇagandhaṃ aheṭhayaṃ
paleti rasamādāya evaṃ gāme munī care

50

na paresaṃ vilomāni na paresaṃ katâkataṃ
attano'va avekkheyya katāni akatāni ca

51

yathā'pi ruciraṃ pupphaṃ vaṇṇavantaṃ agandhakaṃ
evaṃ subhāsitā vācā aphalā hoti akubbato

52

yathā'pi ruciraṃ pupphaṃ vaṇṇavantaṃ sagandhakaṃ
evaṃ subhāsitā vācā saphalā hoti sakubbato

53

yathā'pi puppharāsimhā kayirā mālāguṇe bahū
evaṃ jātena maccena kattabbaṃ kusalaṃ bahuṃ

48

The hedonist who seeks only the blossoms of sensual delights, whose mind is agitated, him the Evil One (Māra) brings under his sway even before his carnal desires are satiated.

49

As the bee takes away the nectar, and departs from the flower without harming its color or fragrance, so let a sage move about in the village.

50

Let the aspirant observe not the perversities of others, nor what others have and have not done; rather should he consider what he has done and what he has yet to do.

51

Like unto a lovely flower which is exquisite in color, yet lacking in fragrance, even so prove futile the well-spoken words of the man who acts not up to them.

52

Like unto a lovely flower of charming color and sweet fragrance, even so prove fruitful the words of him who acts according to them.

53

As many a garland can be strung from a mass of flowers, so should mortal man born in this world perform many wholesome deeds.

54

na pupphagandho paṭivātam eti
na candanaṃ tagaramallikā vā
satañ ca gandho paṭivātam eti
sabbā disā sappuriso pavāti

55

candanaṃ tagaraṃ vā'pi uppalaṃ atha vassikī
etesaṃ gandhajātānaṃ sīlagandho anuttaro

56

appamatto ayaṃ gandho y'āyaṃ tagaracandanī
yo ca sīlavataṃ gandho vāti devesu uttamo

57

tesaṃ sampannasīlānaṃ appamādavihārinaṃ
sammadaññā vimuttānaṃ māro maggaṃ na vindati

58, 59

yathā saṅkāradhānasmiṃ ujjhitasmiṃ mahāpathe
padumaṃ tattha jāyetha sucigandhaṃ manoramaṃ

evaṃ saṅkārabhūtesu andhabhūte puthujjane
atirocati paññāya sammāsambuddhasāvako

54

The fragrance of flowers does not travel against the wind, be it that of sandalwood, tagara, or jasmine. But the fragrance of the virtuous man travels even against the wind. The virtuous man pervades all directions with his purity.

55

Among all the fragrant scents, like sandalwood, tagara, the water lily and the wild jasmine, the fragrance of moral purity is foremost and unique.

56

That scent of sandalwood, tagara plant (and other fragrant things) is of little account; whereas the aroma of the virtuous expands in a greater sphere, even up to the gods.

57

Māra (the Evil One) cannot approach the path of the virtuous, the vigilant, and those who are emancipated through wisdom.

58, 59

As upon a heap of rubbish, thrown on the highway, a lily grows and blooms, fragrant and elegant, so among the ignorant multitudes does the disciple of the Fully Enlightened One shine in resplendent wisdom.

BĀLAVAGGO PAÑCAMO

60

dīghā jāgarato ratti dīghaṃ santassa yojanaṃ
dīgho bālānaṃ saṃsāro saddhammaṃ avijānataṃ

61

carañ ce nâdhigaccheyya seyyaṃ sadisam attano
ekacariyaṃ daḷhaṃ kayirā n'atthi bāle sahāyatā

62

puttā m'atthi dhanam m'atthi iti bālo vihaññati
attā hi attano n'atthi kuto puttā kuto dhanaṃ

63

yo bālo maññati bālyaṃ paṇḍito vā'pi tena so
bālo ca paṇḍitamānī sa ve bālo'ti vuccati

64

yāvajīvampi ce bālo paṇḍitaṃ payirupāsati
na so dhammaṃ vijānāti dabbī sūparasaṃ yathā

The Fool – Canto V

60

Long is the night to a sleepless person; long is the distance of a league to a tired person; long is the circle of rebirths to a fool who does not know the true Law.

61

If a genuine seeker, who sets forth in search of a superior friend, does not come in contact with such a one or at least an equal, then he should resolutely choose the solitary course, for there can be no companionship with the ignorant.

62

"I have children, I have wealth," thinking thus, the fool torments himself. But, when he is not the possessor of his own self, how then of children? How then of wealth?

63

The fool who knows of his ignorance, indeed, through that very consideration becomes a wise man. But that conceited fool who considers himself learned is, in fact, called a fool.

64

A fool who associates with a wise man throughout his life may not know the Dhamma any more than the ladle the taste of soup.

65

muhuttamapi ce viññū paṇḍitaṃ payirupāsati
khippaṃ dhammaṃ vijānāti jivhā sūparasaṃ yathā

66

caranti bālā dummedhā amitten'eva attanā
karontā pāpakaṃ kammaṃ yaṃ hoti kaṭukapphalaṃ

67

na taṃ kammaṃ kataṃ sādhu yaṃ katvā anutappati
yassa assumukho rodaṃ vipākaṃ paṭisevati

68

tañ ca kammaṃ kataṃ sādhu yaṃ katvā nânutappati
yassa patīto sumano vipākaṃ paṭisevati

69

madhū'va maññati bālo yāva pāpaṃ na paccati
yadā ca paccati pāpaṃ atha (bālo) dukkhaṃ nigacchati

70

māse māse kusaggena bālo bhuñjetha bhojanaṃ
na so saṅkhatadhammānaṃ kalaṃ agghati soḷasiṃ

71

na hi pāpaṃ kataṃ kammaṃ sajju khīraṃ'va muccati
ḍahantaṃ bālam anveti bhasmācchanno'va pāvako

65

As the tongue detects the taste of the broth, so the intelligent person who associates with a wise man even for a moment comes to realize the essence of the Law.

66

The unwise, fools who are enemies to themselves, go about committing sinful deeds which produce bitter fruits.

67

Not well done is that deed which one, having performed, has to repent; whose consequence one has to face with tears and lamentation.

68

Well done is that deed which one, having performed, does not repent, and whose consequence one experiences with delight and contentment.

69

So long as an evil deed does not mature (bring disastrous results), the fool thinks his deed to be sweet as honey. But, when his evil deed matures, he falls into untold misery.

70

Though a fool (practicing austerity) may eat his food from the tip of a blade of kuśa grass for months and months, he is not worth one-sixteenth part of those who have realized the Good Law.

71

As fresh-drawn milk from the cow does not soon curdle, so an evil deed does not produce immediate fruits. It follows the wrongdoer like a smoldering spark that burns throughout and then suddenly blazes up.

72

yāvad eva anatthāya ñattaṃ bālassa jāyati
hanti bālassa sukkaṃsaṃ muddham assa vipātayaṃ

73, 74

asataṃ bhāvanam iccheyya purekkhārañ ca bhikkhusu
āvāsesu ca issariyaṃ pūjā parakulesu ca

mam eva kata maññantu gihī pabbajitā ubho
mam ev'ativasā assu kiccākiccesu kismici
iti bālassa saṅkappo icchā māno ca vaḍḍhati

75

aññā hi lābhūpanisā aññā nibbānagāminī
evam etaṃ abhiññāya bhikkhu buddhassa sāvako
sakkāraṃ nâbhinandeyya vivekam anubrūhaye

72

Whatever knowledge a fool acquires causes him only harm. It cleaves his head and destroys his good nature (through conceit).

73, 74

Unwise is the monk who desires undue adoration from others, lordship over other monks, authority among the monastic dwellings and homage even from outside groups. Moreover, he thinks, "May both laymen and monks highly esteem my action! May they be subject to me in all actions, great or small." Such is the grasping desire of a worldly monk whose haughtiness and conceit ever increase.

75

One path leads to worldly gain and honor; quite another path leads to nirvana. Having realized this truth, let not the monk, the true follower of the Enlightened One, yearn for homage from others, but let him cultivate serenity of mind and dispassion.

PAṆḌITAVAGGO CHAṬṬHO

76

nidhīnaṃ'va pavattāraṃ yaṃ passe vajjadassinaṃ
niggayhavādiṃ medhāviṃ tādisaṃ paṇḍitaṃ bhaje
tādisaṃ bhajamānassa seyyo hoti na pāpiyo

77

ovadeyyānusāseyya asabbhā ca nivāraye
sataṃ hi so piyo hoti asataṃ hoti appiyo

78

na bhaje pāpake mitte na bhaje purisâdhame
bhajetha mitte kalyāṇe bhajetha purisuttame

79

dhammapīti sukhaṃ seti vippasannena cetasā
ariyappavedite dhamme sadā ramati paṇḍito

80

udakaṃ hi nayanti nettikā
usukārā namayanti tejanaṃ
dāruṃ namayanti tacchakā
attānaṃ damayanti paṇḍitā

The Wise – Canto VI

76

The disciple should associate with a wise friend, who detects and censures his faults, and who points out virtues as a guide tells of buried treasures. There is happiness, not woe, to him who associates with such an intelligent friend.

77

The man who exhorts, instructs and dissuades his fellow-men from unworthy acts is dear to the virtuous and hated by the wicked.

78

Do not keep company with evildoing friends nor with people who are base; associate with the good, associate with the best of men.

79

One who drinks the nectar of the Good Law lives happily with a tranquil mind. The wise man ever delights in the Dhamma as realized by the Noble Ones.

80

Irrigators conduct the water wherever they wish; fletchers shape the shafts; carpenters work* the wood, and wise men discipline themselves.

*The Pāli verb *namayanti* literally means "bend."

81

selo yathā ekaghano vātena na samīrati
evaṃ nindāpasaṃsāsu na samiñjanti paṇḍitā

82

yathâpi rahado gambhīro vippasanno anāvilo
evaṃ dhammāni sutvāna vippasīdanti paṇḍitā

83

sabbattha ve sappurisā cajanti na kāmakāmā lapayanti santo
sukhena phuṭṭhā athavā dukhena na uccâvacaṃ paṇḍitā dassayanti

84

na attahetu na parassa hetu na puttam icche na dhanaṃ na raṭṭhaṃ
na yicche adhammena samiddhim attano sa sīlavā paññavā dhammiko siyā

85

appakā te manussesu ye janā pāragāmino
athâyaṃ itarā pajā tīram evânudhāvati

86

ye ca kho sammadakkhāte dhamme dhammânuvattino
te janā pāram essanti maccudheyyaṃ suduttaraṃ

87

kaṇhaṃ dhammaṃ vippahāya sukkaṃ bhāvetha paṇḍito
okā anokam āgamma viveke yattha dūramaṃ

81

As a solid rock is not shaken by the wind, so the wise are not shaken by censure or praise.

82

The wise, having hearkened to the Good Law, become serene like unto a deep, calm and crystal-clear lake.

83

Good men abandon lusting after things; they take no pleasure in sensual speech; when touched by happiness or sorrow, the wise show no elation or dejection.

84

For the sake of oneself, or for the sake of another, one should not long for a son, wealth or a kingdom. He who does not crave success or prosperity by wrongful means is indeed virtuous, wise and honorable.

85

Few among men cross over to the further shore; the multitudes who remain run to and fro on this shore.

86

Those who live according to the Dhamma which has been well proclaimed (by the Buddha) will cross over the impassable realm of death to the further shore.

87

Having abandoned the ways of darkness, let the wise follow the light. Having come from home to homelessness, let him enjoy the bliss of solitude, so difficult to achieve.

88

tatrâbhiratim iccheyya hitvā kāme akiñcano
pariyodapeyya attānaṃ cittaklesehi paṇḍito

89

yesaṃ sambodhiyaṅgesu sammā cittaṃ subhāvitaṃ
ādānapaṭinissagge anupādāya ye ratā
khīṇâsavā jutīmanto te loke parinibbutā

88

He should focus his mind upon that exalted state (nirvana). Having given up all sense pleasures, possessing nothing, let the wise, cleansing the mind from defilements, purify the self.

89

Those whose minds are well fixed upon the elements of enlightenment (*sambodhi*),* who, without hankering after anything, glory in renunciation, whose biases are extinguished, who are full of light, they indeed have attained the bliss of nirvana in this very world.

---

*The seven links of *sambodhi* are: 1) mindfulness; 2) wisdom; 3) energy; 4) joyousness; 5) serenity; 6) concentrated meditation; 7) equanimity.

ARAHANTAVAGGO SATTAMO

90

gat'addhino visokassa vippamuttassa sabbadhi
sabbaganthappahīnassa pariḷāho na vijjati

91

uyyuñjanti satīmanto na nikete ramanti te
haṃsā'va pallalaṃ hitvā okam okaṃ jahanti te

92

yesaṃ sannicayo n'atthi ye pariññātabhojanā
suññato animitto ca vimokkho yesaṃ gocaro
ākāse'va sakuntānaṃ gati tesaṃ durannayā

93

yassâsavā parikkhīṇā āhāre ca anissito
suññato animitto ca vimokkho yassa gocaro
ākāse'va sakuntānaṃ padaṃ tassa durannayaṃ

The Holy One – Canto VII

90

The fever of passion afflicts not the holy one (*arahant*), who has completed his samsāric journey (cycle of rebirths), who is free from sorrow, absolutely emancipated, and who has destroyed all knots of attachment.

91

Mindful ones constantly strive, they do not cling to a dwelling place; like swans that abandon a lake, the holy ones abandon house and home.

92

Those who have no accumulation (of worldly possessions), who have a well-regulated diet, who are within range of perfect deliverance through realization of the Void and the conditionlessness of all forms (*suññatā* and *animitta*), their holy path is as difficult to trace as is the track of birds in the air.

93

He whose mental attachments are extinguished, who is not immoderate in food, who is within range of perfect deliverance through realization of the Void and the conditionlessness of all forms, his holy path is as difficult to trace as is the track of birds in the air.

94

yass'indriyāni samathaṅgatāni
assā yathā sārathinā sudantā
pahīnamānassa anāsavassa
devā'pi tassa pihayanti tādino

95

paṭhavīsamo no virujjhati
indakhīlûpamo tādi subbato
rahado'va apetakaddamo
saṃsārā na bhavanti tādino

96

santaṃ tassa manaṃ hoti santā vācā ca kamma ca
sammadaññā vimuttassa upasantassa tādino

97

assaddho akataññū ca sandhicchedo ca yo naro
hatâvakāso vantâso sa ve uttamaporiso

98

gāme vā yadi vâraññe ninne vā yadi vā thale
yatthârahanto viharanti taṃ bhūmiṃ rāmaṇeyyakam

99

ramaṇīyāni araññāni yattha na ramatī jano
vītarāgā ramissanti na te kāmagavesino

94

He whose senses are subdued, like horses well trained by a charioteer, whose pride is destroyed and who is free from corruption, even the gods cherish such a one.

95

He who is unperturbed like the earth, who is steadfast like Indra's post (in the portal of a city), whose character is as pure and translucent as a clear lake, to such a holy one there are no further cycles of rebirth (*saṃsāra*).

96

His mind becomes calm. His word and deed are calm. Such is the state of tranquillity of one who has attained to deliverance through the realization of truth.

97

He who is not credulous, who knows the nature of the Uncreated (*akata*), who has severed all the bonds (of rebirth), who has destroyed all the influxes of evil and given up all cravings, he, indeed, is noblest among men.

98

That spot is truly delightful where the Holy Ones (*arahant*) reside, be it village or forest, valley or high ground.

99

Charming are the forests which do not attract the multitudes. But the holy ones, free from attachments, find delight in them for they are not seekers after the allurements of the senses.

SAHASSAVAGGO AṬṬHAMO

100

sahassam api ce vācā anatthapadasaṃhitā
ekaṃ atthapadaṃ seyyo yaṃ sutvā upasammati

101

sahassam api ce gāthā anatthapadasaṃhitā
ekaṃ gāthāpadaṃ seyyo yaṃ sutvā upasammati

102

yo ca gāthāsataṃ bhāse anatthapadasaṃhitā
ekaṃ dhammapadaṃ seyyo yaṃ sutvā upasammati

103

yo sahassaṃ sahassena saṅgāme mānuse jine
ekañ ca jeyya attānaṃ sa ve saṅgāmajuttamo

104, 105

attā have jitaṃ seyyo yā câyam itarā pajā
attadantassa posassa niccaṃ saṃyatacārino
n'eva devo na gandhabbo na māro saha brahmunā
jitaṃ apajitaṃ kayirā tathārūpassa jantuno

The Thousands — CANTO VIII

100

A single word full of meaning, hearing which one becomes at peace, is better than a thousand words which are empty of meaning.

101

A single couplet pregnant with meaning, hearing which one becomes at peace, is better than a thousand couplets composed of meaningless words.

102

One word of the Dhamma, hearing which one becomes at peace, is better than the utterance of a hundred verses which consist of superficial words.

103

Though one were to conquer a million men in battle, that man who conquers himself is the greater victor.

104, 105

To overcome one's own self is indeed better than to conquer others.

Neither god nor demigod, nor Māra with Brahmā, can undo the victory of him who has subjugated himself and who practices self-restraint.

106

māse māse sahassena yo yajetha sataṃ samaṃ
ekañ ca bhāvitattānaṃ muhuttam api pūjaye
sā yeva pūjanā seyyo yañ ce vassasataṃ hutaṃ

107

yo ca vassasataṃ jantu aggiṃ paricare vane
ekañ ca bhāvitattānaṃ muhuttam api pūjaye
sā yeva pūjanā seyyo yañ ce vassasataṃ hutaṃ

108

yaṃ kiñci yiṭṭhaṃ va hutaṃ va loke
saṃvaccharaṃ yajetha puññapekkho
sabbampi taṃ na catubhāgam eti
abhivādanā ujjugatesu seyyo

109

abhivādanasīlissa niccaṃ vaḍḍhâpacāyino
cattāro dhammā vaḍḍhanti āyu vaṇṇo sukham balaṃ

110

yo ca vassasataṃ jīve dussīlo asamāhito
ekâhaṃ jīvitaṃ seyyo sīlavantassa jhāyino

111

yo ca vassasataṃ jīve duppañño asamāhito
ekâhaṃ jīvitaṃ seyyo paññāvantassa jhāyino

106

Were a man month after month for a hundred years to offer sacrifices by the thousands, and were he to pay homage even for a moment to one who is self-governed, that homage is superior to the sacrifices of a hundred years.

107

Were a man for a hundred years to tend the sacrificial fire in the forest, and were he to pay homage even for a moment to one who is self-governed, that homage is superior to the fire-sacrifice of a hundred years.

108

Whatever offering or sacrifice a person, who is desirous of gaining merit, may make throughout the course of a year, that is not worth one fourth of the merit acquired by homage paid to one of upright life.

109

In him, who always honors and respects the aged, four conditions will increase: longevity, beauty, happiness and strength.

110

One day's life of an Arhat who is virtuous and contemplative is better than a hundred years of life of one who is dissolute and of uncontrolled mind.

111

One day's life of him who is wise and contemplative is better than a life of a hundred years of one who is unwise and of uncontrolled mind.

112

yo ca vassasataṃ jīve kusīto hīnavīriyo
ekâhaṃ jīvitaṃ seyyo viriyaṃ ārabhato daḷhaṃ

113

yo ca vassasataṃ jīve apassaṃ udayavyayaṃ
ekâhaṃ jīvitaṃ seyyo passato udayavyayaṃ

114

yo ca vassasataṃ jīve apassaṃ amataṃ padaṃ
ekâhaṃ jīvitaṃ seyyo passato amataṃ padaṃ

115

yo ca vassasataṃ jīve apassaṃ dhammamuttamaṃ
ekâhaṃ jīvitaṃ seyyo passato dhammamuttamaṃ

112

One day's life of a person who is vigorous and resolute is better than a life of a hundred years of him who is weak and indolent.

113

A single day's life of one who clearly sees the origin and cessation (of all composite things), is better than a hundred years of life of him who does not perceive the origin and cessation of things.

114

A single day's life of one who perceives the immortal state is far better than if one were to live a hundred years without perceiving this state.

115

A single day's life of one who realizes the Sublime Truth is indeed better than a life of a hundred years of one who does not realize the Sublime Truth.

PĀPAVAGGO NAVAMO

116

abhittharetha kalyāṇe pāpā cittaṃ nivāraye
dandhaṃ hi karoto puññaṃ pāpasmiṃ ramatī mano

117

pāpañ ce puriso kayirā na taṃ kayirā punappunaṃ
na tamhi chandaṃ kayirātha dukkho pāpassa uccayo

118

puññañ ce puriso kayirā kayirāth'enam punappunaṃ
tamhi chandaṃ kayirātha sukho puññassa uccayo

119

pāpo'pi passati bhadraṃ yāva pāpaṃ na paccati
yadā ca paccati pāpaṃ atha pāpo pāpāni passati

120

bhadro'pi passati pāpaṃ yāva bhadraṃ na paccati
yadā ca paccati bhadraṃ atha bhadro bhadrāni passati

Evil – Canto IX

116

Make haste in doing good and restrain the mind from evil; if one is slow in doing good, the mind finds delight in evil.

117

If a man commits evil let him not repeat it again and again; let him not delight in it, for the accumulation of sin brings suffering.

118

If a man commits a meritorious deed, let him perform it again and again; let him develop a longing for doing good; happiness is the outcome of the accumulation of merit.

119

Even the wrongdoer finds some happiness so long as (the fruit of) his misdeed does not mature; but when it does mature, then he sees its evil results.

120

Even the doer of good deeds knows evil (days) so long as his merit has not matured; but when his merit has fully matured, then he sees the happy results of his meritorious deeds.

121

mā'ppamaññetha pāpassa na man taṃ āgamissati
udabindunipātena udakumbho pi pūrati
pūrati bālo pāpassa thokathokam pi ācinaṃ

122

mā'ppamaññetha puññassa na man taṃ āgamissati
udabindunipātena udakumbho pi pūrati
pūrati dhīro puññassa thokathokam pi ācinaṃ

123

vāṇijo'va bhayaṃ maggaṃ appasattho mahaddhano
visaṃ jīvitukāmo'va pāpāni parivajjaye

124

pāṇimhi ce vaṇo nâssa hareyya pāṇinā visaṃ
nābbaṇaṃ visam anveti n'atthi pāpaṃ akubbato

125

yo appaduṭṭhassa narassa dussati
suddhassa posassa anaṅgaṇassa
tam eva bālaṃ pacceti pāpaṃ
sukhumo rajo paṭivātaṃ'va khitto

126

gabbham eke uppajjanti nirayaṃ pāpakammino
saggaṃ sugatino yanti parinibbanti anāsavā

121

Do not think lightly of evil, saying, "It will not come to me." By the constant fall of waterdrops, a pitcher is filled; likewise the unwise person, accumulating evil little by little, becomes full of evil.

122

Do not think lightly of merit, saying, "It will not come to me." By the constant fall of waterdrops, a pitcher is filled; likewise the wise person, accumulating merit little by little, becomes full of merit.

123

As a merchant who has limited escort, yet carries much wealth, avoids a perilous road, as a man who is desirous of living long avoids poison, so in the same way should the wise shun evil.

124

If one does not have a wound in his hand, he may carry poison in his palm. Poison does not affect him who has no wound. There is no ill effect for the person who does no wrong.

125

Whoever offends an innocent, pure and faultless person, the evil (of his act) rebounds on that fool, even as fine dust thrown against the wind.

126

(After death), some are reborn in the womb; evildoers are born in hell; those who commit meritorious deeds go to heaven; and those who are free from worldly desires realize nirvana.

127

na antalikkhe na samuddamajjhe
na pabbatānaṃ vivaraṃ pavissa
na vijjatī so jagatippadeso
yatthaṭṭhito muñceyya pāpakammā

128

na antalikkhe na samuddamajjhe
na pabbatānaṃ vivaraṃ pavissa
na vijjatī so jagatippadeso
yatthaṭṭhitaṃ nappasahetha maccu

127

Not in the sky, not in the middle of the ocean, not even in the cave of a mountain, should one seek refuge, for there exists no place in the world where one can escape the effects of wrongdoing.

128

Not in the sky, not in the middle of the ocean, not even in the cave of a mountain, should one seek refuge, for there exists no place in the world where one will not be overpowered by death.

DAṆḌAVAGGO DASAMO

129

sabbe tasanti daṇḍassa sabbe bhāyanti maccuno
attānaṃ upamaṃ katvā na haneyya na ghātaye

130

sabbe tasanti daṇḍassa sabbesaṃ jīvitaṃ piyaṃ
attānaṃ upamaṃ katvā na haneyya na ghātaye

131

sukhakāmāni bhūtāni yo daṇḍena vihiṃsati
attano sukhamesāno pecca so na labhate sukhaṃ

132

sukhakāmāni bhūtāni yo daṇḍena na hiṃsati
attano sukhamesāno pecca so labhate sukhaṃ

133

mā'voca pharusaṃ kañci vuttā paṭivadeyyu taṃ
dukkhā hi sārambhakathā paṭidaṇḍā phuseyyu taṃ

The Rod of Punishment – CANTO X

129

All tremble before the rod of punishment; all fear death; likening others to oneself, one should neither slay nor cause to slay.

130

All tremble before the rod of punishment; for all life is dear; likening others to oneself, one should neither slay nor cause to slay.

131

He who, desirous of happiness for himself, torments with a rod others who are likewise seeking enjoyment, shall not obtain happiness in the hereafter.

132

He who, desirous of happiness for himself, does not torment others who likewise long for happiness, shall obtain happiness in the hereafter.

133

Do not speak harshly to anyone; those thus spoken to will retaliate in kind; discordant indeed will be the response, and soon retribution will overtake you.

134

sace neresi attānaṃ kaṃso upahato yathā
esa patto'si nibbānaṃ sārambho te na vijjati

135

yathā daṇḍena gopālo gāvo pāceti gocaraṃ
evaṃ jarā ca maccū ca āyuṃ pācenti pāṇinaṃ

136

atha pāpāni kammāni karaṃ bālo na bujjhati
sehi kammehi dummedho aggidaḍḍho'va tappati

137

yo daṇḍena adaṇḍesu appaduṭṭhesu dussati
dasannam aññataraṃ ṭhānaṃ khippam eva nigacchati

138, 139, 140

vedanaṃ pharusaṃ jāniṃ sarīrassa ca bhedanaṃ
garukaṃ vā'pi ābādhaṃ cittakkhepañ ca pāpuṇe
rājato vā upassaggaṃ abbhakkhānañ ca dāruṇaṃ
parikkhayaṃ va ñātīnaṃ bhogānañ ca pabhaṅguraṃ
athav'assa agārāni aggi ḍahati pāvako
kāyassa bhedā duppañño nirayaṃ so'papajjati

141

na naggacariyā na jaṭā na paṅkā
nânāsakā thaṇḍilasāyikā vā
rajo'va jall'ukkuṭikappadhānaṃ
sodhenti maccaṃ avitiṇṇakaṅkhaṃ

134

If you can make yourself as silent as a shattered bronze gong, then you have attained to the peace of nirvana, for now there is no discord in you.

135

As a cowherd with his rod drives cattle to the pasture, so do old age and death drive the lives of sentient beings.

136

When a person ignorant (of the Dhamma) commits evil deeds, he does not realize their nature. The stupid man burns (suffers) through these deeds as if consumed by fire.

137

He who inflicts punishment upon those who do not deserve it, and hurts those who are harmless, such a person will soon come to face one of these ten states:

138, 139, 140

He may soon come to terrible pain, great deprivations, physical injury, deep-rooted ailment or mental disorder, the wrath of the monarch or a dreadful accusation, loss of relatives, the complete destruction of wealth, or a sudden fire may break out and burn his houses. After the dissolution of his physical body, he will surely be born in hell.

141

Neither nakedness, nor matted locks; neither applying mud (all over the body), nor fasting, nor lying on the bare earth; neither besmearing oneself with soot, nor squatting on one's heels, can purify a man who has not got rid of his doubts.

142

alaṅkato ce'pi samañ careyya
santo danto niyato brahmacārī
sabbesu bhūtesu nidhāya daṇḍaṃ
so brāhmaṇo so samaṇo sa bhikkhu

143

hirīnisedho puriso koci lokasmiṃ vijjati
yo nindaṃ appabodhati asso bhadro kasāmiva

144

asso yathā bhadro kasāniviṭṭho
ātāpino saṃvegino bhavātha
saddhāya sīlena ca viriyena ca
samādhinā dhammavinicchayena ca
sampannavijjācaraṇā paṭissatā
pahassatha dukkham idaṃ anappakaṃ

145

udakaṃ hi nayanti nettikā
usukārā namayanti tejanaṃ
dāruṃ namayanti tacchakā
attānaṃ damayanti subbatā

142

Even though a person be dressed in fine clothes, if he develops tranquillity, is quiet, self-disciplined, resolute and practices celibacy, and abstains from injuring all other beings, he is indeed a Brāhman, an ascetic and a monk.

143

Is there any man in this world so self-restrained through modesty that he avoids censure as a self-respecting horse avoids the whip?

144

As a well-trained horse when touched by the whip, even so be you strenuous and eager. By devotion, virtue, effort, concentration, and by the critical investigation of truth (*dhamma*) may you abandon this great suffering (of *saṃsāra*), perfect in wisdom, conduct and awareness.

145

Irrigators conduct water wherever they wish; fletchers shape the shafts; carpenters work the wood, and wise men discipline themselves.

JARĀVAGGO EKĀDASAMO

146

ko nu hāso kim ānando niccaṃ pajjalite sati
andhakārena onaddhā padīpaṃ na gavessatha

147

passa cittakataṃ bimbaṃ arukāyaṃ samussitaṃ
āturaṃ bahusaṅkappaṃ yassa n'atthi dhuvaṃ ṭhiti

148

parijiṇṇam idaṃ rūpaṃ roganiḍḍhaṃ pabhaṅguraṃ
bhijjati pūtisandeho maraṇantaṃ hi jīvitaṃ

149

yāni'māni apatthāni alāpun'eva sārade
kāpotakāni aṭṭhīni tāni disvāna kā rati

150

aṭṭhīnaṃ nagaraṃ kataṃ maṃsalohitalepanaṃ
yattha jarā ca maccū ca māno makkho ca ohito

151

jīranti ve rājarathā sucittā
atho sarīrampi jaraṃ upeti

Old Age – CANTO XI

146

Why laugh, why be jubilant, when all is constantly burning (with desires)? Should you not seek the light of wisdom when you are enveloped by the darkness of ignorance?

147

Behold this illusory human image, embellished (by rich attire and jewels), full of corruptions, a structure of bones, liable to constant illness, full of countless hankerings, in which there is nothing permanent or stable.

148

This frail form is a nest of diseases. It is fragile and putrid. It disintegrates and death is the end of life.

149

These dove-grey bones are like unto the gourds thrown away in the autumnal season. What pleasure is there in looking at them?

150

Here is a citadel built of bones, plastered with flesh and blood, wherein are concealed decay, death, vanity and deceit.

151

The gaily decorated royal chariots wear out. So likewise does this body. But the truth of the righteous does not wear

satañ ca dhammo na jaraṃ upeti
santo have sabbhi pavedayanti

152
appassutâyaṃ puriso balivaddo'va jīrati
maṃsāni tassa vaḍḍhanti paññā tassa na vaḍḍhati

153
anekajātisaṃsāraṃ sandhāvissaṃ anibbisaṃ
gahakārakaṃ gavesanto dukkhā jāti punappunaṃ

154
gahakāraka diṭṭho'si puna gehaṃ na kāhasi
sabbā te phāsukā bhaggā gahakūṭaṃ visaṅkhitaṃ
visaṅkhāragataṃ cittaṃ taṇhānaṃ khayam ajjhagā

155
acaritvā brahmacariyaṃ aladdhā yobbane dhanaṃ
jiṇṇakoñcā'va jhāyanti khīṇamacche'va pallale

156
acaritvā brahmacariyaṃ aladdhā yobbane dhanaṃ
senti cāpâtikhīṇā'va purāṇāni anutthunaṃ

out with age. Thus do the enlightened proclaim it to the wise.

152

The man of little spiritual learning grows like an ox; his flesh increases, but his wisdom does not.

153

For countless births have I passed through this cycle of births and deaths, seeking the builder of this tabernacle, but in vain. Sorrowful indeed is this cyclic repetition of births.

154

O builder of the house, I have seen you; you shall not build the house again. All the rafters are broken; the ridge-pole is sundered. Mind has arrived at dissolution (nirvana), having attained the extinction of all cravings (*tanhā*).

155

Those who do not practice self-discipline, who do not acquire wealth in their youth, when they become old, pine away, like old herons in a dried-up lake where there are no fish.

156

Those who do not practice self-discipline, who do not acquire wealth in their youth, lie like broken arrows, lamenting the deeds of the past.

ATTAVAGGO DVĀDASAMO

157

attānañ ce piyaṃ jaññā rakkheyya naṃ surakkhitaṃ
tiṇṇam aññataraṃ yāmaṃ paṭijaggeyya paṇḍito

158

attānam eva paṭhamaṃ patirūpe nivesaye
ath'aññam anusāseyya na kilisseyya paṇḍito

159

attānañ ce tathā kayirā yath'aññam anusāsati
sudanto vata dametha attā hi kira duddamo

160

attā hi attano nātho ko hi nātho paro siyā
attanā hi sudantena nāthaṃ labhati dullabhaṃ

161

attanā'va kataṃ pāpaṃ attajam atta sambhavam
abhimanthati dummedhaṃ vajiraṃ v'asmamayam maṇim

The Self – Canto XII

157

If a man esteems the self, let him guard himself with great care. Let the wise man keep vigil over himself, in one of the three watches (of life or of the night).

158

Let each first firmly establish himself in right conduct, then only may he admonish others. Such a wise man does not suffer blemish.

159

Let a man mold himself into what he admonishes others to be. Thus well-controlled he can control others. It is extremely difficult indeed to control one's own self.

160

The self is the master of the self. Who else can that master be? With the self fully subdued, one obtains the sublime refuge which is very difficult to achieve.

161

The sin committed by oneself, born of oneself, produced by oneself, crushes the evil-minded one as the diamond cuts the precious stone.

162

yassa accantadussīlyaṃ māluvā sālam iv'otthataṃ
karoti so tath'attānam yathā naṃ icchati diso

163

sukarāni asādhūni attano ahitāni ca
yaṃ ve hitañ ca sādhuñ ca taṃ ve paramadukkaraṃ

164

yo sāsanaṃ arahataṃ ariyānaṃ dhamma jīvinaṃ
paṭikkosati dummedho diṭṭhiṃ nissāya pāpikaṃ
phalāni kaṭṭhakasseva attaghaññāya phallati

165

attanā'va kataṃ pāpaṃ attanā saṅkilissati
attanā akataṃ pāpaṃ attanā'va visujjhati
suddhi asuddhi paccattaṃ nâñño aññaṃ visodhaye

166

attadatthaṃ paratthena bahunā'pi na hāpaye
attadatthaṃ abhiññāya sadatthapasuto siyā

162

As the parasitic māluvā creeper destroys the sal tree which it entwines, so the immoral conduct of a man gradually makes of him what his enemy would have him be.

163

It is quite easy to perform evil deeds which are not beneficial to oneself. But it is extremely difficult to perform a deed which is righteous and beneficial.

164

If an evil-minded one, by reason of his false views, reviles the teaching of the Arhats, the Noble Ones, and the virtuous, verily he brings forth the fruit of his own destruction, even as does the katthaka reed.

165

By self alone is evil done; by self alone is one defiled; by self alone is evil not done; by self alone is one purified. Purity and impurity depend on oneself; no one can purify another.

166

However much one is engaged in activities for the good of others, one should not neglect his own (spiritual) purpose. Having discerned one's own task, let him apply himself to that task with diligence.

LOKAVAGGO TERASAMO

167

hīnaṃ dhammaṃ na seveyya pamādena na saṃvase
micchādiṭṭhiṃ na seveyya na siyā lokavaddhano

168

uttiṭṭhe nappamajjeyya dhammaṃ sucaritaṃ care
dhammacārī sukhaṃ seti asmiṃ loke paramhi ca

169

dhammaṃ care sucaritaṃ na naṃ duccaritaṃ care
dhammacārī sukhaṃ seti asmiṃ loke paramhi ca

170

yathā bubbulakaṃ passe yathā passe marīcikaṃ
evaṃ lokaṃ avekkhantaṃ maccurājā na passati

171

etha passath'imaṃ lokaṃ cittaṃ rājarathûpamaṃ
yattha bālā visīdanti n'atthi saṅgo vijānataṃ

The World – Canto XIII

167

Let no one follow a degraded course of existence, nor live in indolence; let him not follow false views, nor be a person who prolongs his worldly existence.

168

Awake! Be not heedless. Follow the truth (*dhamma*). He who embarks upon the path of truth lives happily in this world and in the hereafter.

169

Follow the law of morality; do not follow the law of immorality; he who embarks upon the path of truth lives happily in this world and in the hereafter.

170

Look upon the world as a bubble, regard it as a mirage; who thus perceives the world, him Māra, the king of death, does not see.

171

Come, behold this world, resplendent like unto a royal chariot. Fools are immersed in it; but the wise have no attachment for it.

172

yo ca pubbe pamajjitvā pacchā so nappamajjati
so imaṃ lokaṃ pabhāseti abbhā mutto'va candimā

173

yassa pāpaṃ kataṃ kammaṃ kusalena pithīyati
so imaṃ lokaṃ pabhāseti abbhā mutto'va candimā

174

andhabhūto ayaṃ loko tanuk'ettha vipassati
sakunto jālamutto'va appo saggāya gacchati

175

haṃsâdiccapathe yanti ākāse yanti iddhiyā
nīyanti dhīrā lokamhā jetvā māraṃ savāhiniṃ

176

ekaṃ dhammaṃ atītassa musāvādissa jantuno
vitiṇṇaparalokassa n'atthi pāpaṃ akāriyaṃ

177

na ve kadariyā devalokaṃ vajanti
bālā have nappasaṃsanti dānaṃ
dhīro ca dānaṃ anumodamāno
ten'eva so hoti sukhī parattha

178

pathavyā ekarajjena saggassa gamanena vā
sabbalokādhipaccena sotāpattiphalaṃ varaṃ

172

He who formerly was heedless, but, after due consideration, becomes vigilant, illumines the world as the moon freed from a cloud.

173

He whose evil deeds are superseded by meritorious deeds, illumines the world as the moon freed from a cloud.

174

This world is blind. Few are they who can see things as they are. As birds escaped from the net, few go to heaven.

175

Swans fly in the path of the sun; those who possess psychic powers (*iddhi*) go through the air. The wise, having conquered Māra and his hosts, go forth out of this world.

176

There is no sin that a man will not commit who utters falsehood, who has transgressed the one law of truthfulness (*dhamma*), and who has rejected the other world.

177

Indeed the miserly do not go to the world of the gods; the foolish do not praise liberality. But the wise man who takes pleasure in giving, through that very act becomes happy in the next world.

178

The fruit of entering the stream (the path) is superior to that of the sole sovereignty of the world, or going to heaven, or the supreme lordship over the whole universe.

BUDDHAVAGGO CUDDASAMO

179

yassa jitaṃ nāvajīyati jitam'assa no yāti koci loke
taṃ buddhaṃ anantagocaraṃ apadaṃ kena padena nessatha

180

yassa jālinī visattikā taṇhā n'atthi kuhiñci netave
taṃ buddhaṃ anantagocaraṃ apadaṃ kena padena nessatha

181

ye jhānapasutā dhīrā nekkhammûpasame ratā
devā'pi tesaṃ pihayanti sambuddhānaṃ satīmataṃ

182

kiccho manussapaṭilābho kicchaṃ maccāna jīvitaṃ
kicchaṃ saddhammasavaṇaṃ kiccho buddhānaṃ uppādo

183

sabbapāpassa akaraṇaṃ kusalassa upasampadā
sacittapariyodapanaṃ etaṃ buddhāna sāsanaṃ

The Enlightened One – CANTO XIV

179

By what path will you lead the Buddha of infinite range of perception, the Pathless One, whose conquest of passions cannot be undone, into whose conquest no one in this world enters?

180

By what path will you lead the Buddha of infinite range of perception, the Pathless One, in whom there is not that entangling and poisonous craving which leads one astray (to another state of birth)?

181

Those wise ones who are absorbed in meditation, who take delight in the inner calm of renunciation, such mindful and perfectly awakened ones even the devas (gods) hold dear.

182

Difficult is it to be born as a human being; difficult is the existence of mortals; difficult is the hearing of the Sublime Truth; rare is the appearance of the Enlightened Ones (Buddhas).

183

Abstention from all evil, the doing of good deeds, and the purification of the mind, is the admonition of the Enlightened Ones.

184

khantī paramaṃ tapo titikkhā nibbānaṃ paramaṃ
vadanti buddhā
na hi pabbajito parūpaghātī na samaṇo hoti paraṃ
viheṭhayanto

185

anūpavādo anūpaghāto pāṭimokkhe ca saṃvaro
mattaññutā ca bhattasmiṃ panthañ ca sayanāsanaṃ
adhicitte ca āyogo etaṃ buddhāna sāsanaṃ

186, 187

na kahāpaṇavassena titti kāmesu vijjati
appassādā dukkhā kāmā iti viññāya paṇḍito
api dibbesu kāmesu ratiṃ so nâdhigacchati
taṇhakkhayarato hoti sammāsambuddhasāvako

188

bahuṃ ve saraṇaṃ yanti pabbatāni vanāni ca
ārāmarukkhacetyāni manussā bhayatajjitā

189

n'etaṃ kho saraṇaṃ khemaṃ n'etaṃ saraṇam uttamaṃ
n'etam saraṇam āgamma sabbadukkhā pamuccati

190

yo ca buddhañ ca dhammañ ca saṅghañ ca saraṇaṃ gato
cattāri ariyasaccāni sammappaññāya passati

184

Forbearance which is long-suffering is the highest austerity. The Buddhas declare nirvana to be the supreme state. Verily he is not an anchorite who harms another; nor is he an ascetic who causes grief to another.

185

Not reviling, not injuring, practicing restraint according to the moral code (*pāṭimokkha*) leading to freedom, moderation in eating, living in solitude, dwelling with diligence on the highest thoughts – this is the teaching of the Buddhas.

186, 187

There is no satisfying the passions even by a shower of gold coins; the wise man, knowing that sense delights are of fleeting pleasure and productive of pain, finds no joy even in celestial pleasures. The true disciple of the Fully Enlightened One delights only in the destruction of all worldly desires.

188

Men driven by fear betake themselves to numerous refuges, such as mountains, forests, groves, sacred trees and shrines.

189

Verily, none of these is a safe refuge, nor is it the supreme refuge. For even after arriving at a refuge, one is not emancipated from all suffering.

190

He who takes refuge in the Enlightened One (*buddha*), in his Doctrine (*dhamma*), and in his Community of Monks (*saṅgha*), perceives with clarity of wisdom the Four Noble Truths, namely:

191, 192

dukkhaṃ dukkhasamuppādaṃ dukkhassa ca atikkamaṃ
ariyañ c'aṭṭhaṅgikaṃ maggaṃ dukkhūpasamagāminaṃ

etaṃ kho saraṇaṃ khemaṃ etaṃ saraṇam uttamaṃ
etaṃ saraṇam āgamma sabbadukkhā pamuccati

193

dullabho purisâjañño na so sabbattha jāyati
yattha so jāyati dhīro taṃ kulaṃ sukham edhati

194

sukho buddhānaṃ uppādo sukhā saddhammadesanā
sukhā saṅghassa sāmaggī samaggānaṃ tapo sukho

195, 196

pūjârahe pūjayato buddhe yadi va sāvake
papañcasamatikkante tiṇṇasokapariddave

te tādise pūjayato nibbute akutobhaye
na sakkā puññaṃ saṅkhātuṃ im'ettam api kena ci

191, 192

Suffering, the Origin of Suffering, the Cessation of Suffering, the Noble Eightfold Path* that leads to the cessation of suffering.

That, verily, is the safe refuge and the supreme refuge. After having arrived at that refuge, a man is emancipated from all suffering.

193

An illumined person (a Buddha) is indeed very rare. He is not born everywhere. Wherever such a one takes birth, that family prospers.

194

Blessed is the birth of the Buddhas; blessed is the discourse on the Noble Law; blessed is the harmony of the Community of Monks; blessed is the devotion of those living in brotherhood.

195, 196

He who pays homage to those who deserve homage, whether the Enlightened Ones or their disciples; he who has overcome the host of passions, and crossed the stream of grief and lamentations; he who pays homage to such as are emancipated and fearless – his merit cannot be measured.

---

*See Glossary for detailed list (p. 165).

SUKHAVAGGO PANNARASAMO

197

susukhaṃ vata jīvāma verinesu averino
verinesu manussesu viharāma averino

198

susukhaṃ vata jīvāma āturesu anāturā
āturesu manussesu viharāma anāturā

199

susukhaṃ vata jīvāma ussukesu anussukā
ussukesu manussesu viharāma anussukā

200

susukhaṃ vata jīvāma yesaṃ no n'atthi kiñcanaṃ
pītibhakkhā bhavissāma devā ābhassarā yathā

201

jayaṃ veraṃ pasavati dukkhaṃ seti parâjito
upasanto sukhaṃ seti hitvā jayaparājayaṃ

Happiness – CANTO XV

197

Blessed indeed are we who live among those who hate, hating no one; amidst those who hate, let us dwell without hatred.

198

Blessed indeed are we who live among those who are ailing, without ailments; amidst those who are so afflicted, let us live in good health.

199

Blessed indeed are we who live among those who are yearning for sense delights, without yearning for such things; amidst those who are yearning for sense delights, let us dwell without yearning.

200

Happy indeed are we who live without possessions. Let us feed on happiness, like the radiant gods (who feed on spiritual bliss).

201

Victory breeds enmity; the vanquished one dwells in sorrow; the composed person lives happily, disregarding both victory and defeat.

202

n'atthi rāgasamo aggi n'atthi dosasamo kali
n'atthi khandhādisā dukkhā n'atthi santiparaṃ sukhaṃ

203

jighacchā paramā rogā saṅkhārā paramā dukkhā
etaṃ ñatvā yathābhūtaṃ nibbānaṃ paramaṃ sukhaṃ

204

ārogyaparamā lābhā santuṭṭhiparamaṃ dhanaṃ
vissāsaparamā ñāti nibbānaṃ paramaṃ sukhaṃ

205

pavivekarasaṃ pītvā rasaṃ upasamassa ca
niddaro hoti nippāpo dhammapītirasaṃ pibaṃ

206

sādhu dassanam ariyānaṃ sannivāso sadā sukho
adassanena bālānaṃ niccam eva sukhī siyā

207

bālasaṅgatacārī hi dīgham addhāna socati
dukkho bālehi saṃvāso amitten'eva sabbadā
dhīro ca sukhasaṃvāso ñātīnaṃ va samāgamo

202

There is no fire like passion; there is no blemish like hatred; there is no suffering like physical existence (the five aggregates or skandhas) and there is no bliss equal to the calm (of nirvana).

203

Greed is the worst of afflictions; mental and emotional tendencies are the greatest of sorrows. Having perceived this fact truly, one realizes nirvana, the highest bliss.

204

Health is the greatest of gifts, contentment the greatest of riches; trust is the finest of relationships and nirvana the highest bliss.

205

Having tasted the sweetness of solitude and of inner tranquillity, he becomes free of woe and sin, enjoying the sweetness of the bliss of the Dhamma.

206

Glorious is it to see the Noble Ones; their company at all times brings happiness; by not seeing the spiritually ignorant, one will always be happy.

207

He who leads a life in the company of fools suffers long; it is as painful to live with fools as it is with a foe; association with the wise brings happiness as does the company of one's kinsfolk.

208

dhīrañ ca paññañ ca bahussutañ ca
dhorayhasīlaṃ vatavantam ariyaṃ
taṃ tādisaṃ sappurisaṃ sumedhaṃ
bhajetha nakkhattapathaṃ'va candimā

208

Therefore, one should follow the steadfast, the wise, the educated, the self-reliant, the dutiful and the noble. Even as the moon follows the path of the stars, so ought one to follow such a virtuous and highly intelligent man.

PIYAVAGGO SOLASAMO

209

ayoge yuñjam attānaṃ yogasmiñ ca ayojayaṃ
atthaṃ hitvā piyaggāhī pihet'attānuyoginaṃ

210

mā piyehi samāgañchi appiyehi kudācanaṃ
piyānaṃ adassanaṃ dukkhaṃ appiyānañ ca dassanaṃ

211

tasmā piyaṃ na kayirātha piyâpāyo hi pāpako
ganthā tesaṃ na vijjanti yesaṃ n'atthi piyâppiyaṃ

212

piyato jāyatī soko piyato jāyatī bhayaṃ
piyato vippamuttassa n'atthi soko kuto bhayaṃ

213

pemato jāyatī soko pemato jāyatī bhayaṃ
pemato vippamuttassa n'atthi soko kuto bhayaṃ

214

ratiyā jāyatī soko ratiyā jāyatī bhayaṃ
ratiyā vippamuttassa n'atthi soko kuto bhayaṃ

Affection — CANTO XVI

209

He who gives himself to what is not befitting and thus forgets his own quest; he who indulges in sense pleasures envies the person who exerts himself in meditation.

210

Do not become attached to what is pleasing nor to what is displeasing; not to see what is dear to one is painful, as also is the sight of the unpleasant.

211

Therefore, let no one cherish anything, inasmuch as the loss of what is beloved is hard. There are no fetters for him who knows neither pleasure nor pain.

212

From pleasure arises sorrow; from pleasure arises fear. To him who is free from pleasure there is no sorrow. Whence, then, comes fear?

213

From affection arises sorrow; from affection arises fear. To him who is free from affection there is no sorrow. Whence fear?

214

From attachment arises sorrow; from attachment arises fear. To him who is free from attachment there is no sorrow. Whence fear?

215

kāmato jāyatī soko kāmato jāyatī bhayaṃ
kāmato vippamuttassa n'atthi soko kuto bhayaṃ

216

taṇhāya jāyatī soko taṇhāya jāyatī bhayaṃ
taṇhāya vippamuttassa n'atthi soko kuto bhayaṃ

217

sīladassanasampannaṃ dhammaṭṭhaṃ saccavādinaṃ
attano kamma kubbānaṃ taṃ jano kurute piyaṃ

218

chandajāto anakkhāte manasā ca phuṭo siyā
kāmesu ca appaṭibaddhacitto uddhaṃsoto'ti vuccati

219

cirappavāsiṃ purisaṃ dūrato sotthim āgataṃ
ñātimittā suhajjā ca abhinandanti āgataṃ

220

tath'eva katapuññam pi asmā lokā paraṃ gataṃ
puññāni paṭigaṇhanti piyaṃ ñātī va āgataṃ

215

From desire arises sorrow, from desire arises fear. To him who is free from desire there is no sorrow. Whence fear?

216

From craving arises sorrow; from craving arises fear. To him who is free from craving there is no sorrow. Whence fear?

217

He who possesses virtue and spiritual insight, who is well established in the Dhamma, who is truthful, who performs his duties, him the people hold dear.

218

He in whom is born a sublime longing for the Ineffable, whose mind is permeated by this longing, whose thoughts are not bewildered by attachment — such a person is called "one bound upstream."

219

When a man who has been away for a long time returns home safely, his kinsmen, friends and well-wishers welcome him gladly.

220

When a man has departed from this world to the next, the effects of his good deeds receive him gladly, even as kinsmen welcome a friend on his return home.

KODHAVAGGO SATTARASAMO

221

kodhaṃ jahe vippajaheyya mānaṃ
saññojanaṃ sabbam atikkameyya
taṃ nāmarūpasmiṃ asajjamānaṃ
akiñcanaṃ nânupatanti dukkhā

222

yo ve uppatitaṃ kodhaṃ rathaṃ bhantaṃ va dhāraye
tam ahaṃ sārathiṃ brūmi rasmiggāho itaro jano

223

akkodhena jine kodhaṃ asādhuṃ sādhunā jine
jine kadariyaṃ dānena saccena alikavādinaṃ

224

saccaṃ bhaṇe na kujjheyya dajjā'ppasmimpi yācito
etehi tīhi ṭhānehi gacche devāna santike

225

ahiṃsakā ye munayo niccaṃ kāyena saṃvutā
te yanti accutaṃ ṭhānaṃ yattha gantvā na socare

Anger – Canto XVII

221

Let a man abandon anger, let him renounce pride and let him get beyond all worldly fetters. No suffering befalls him who is passionless and clings neither to mind nor to form (*nāma-rūpa*).

222

He who controls his rising anger as a skilled driver curbs a rolling chariot, him I call a true charioteer. Others merely hold the reins.

223

Let a man conquer anger by love, let him subdue evil by good; let him overcome the greedy by liberality and the liar by truth.

224

One should always speak the truth, not yield to anger, and give, even though it be little, to the person who begs. By these three virtues, a man is able to come into the presence of the devas.

225

Those sages who observe nonviolence, who are ever controlled in body, attain the changeless state (nirvana) where, having gone, they suffer no more.

226

sadā jāgaramānānaṃ ahorattânusikkhinaṃ
nibbānaṃ adhimuttānaṃ atthaṃ gacchanti āsavā

227

porāṇaṃ etaṃ atula n'etaṃ ajjatanām iva
nindanti tuṇhim āsīnaṃ nindanti bahubhāṇinaṃ
mitabhāṇinampi nindanti n'atthi loke anindito

228

na câhu na ca bhavissati na c'etarahi vijjati
ekantaṃ nindito poso ekantaṃ vā pasaṃsito

229, 230

yañ ce viññū pasaṃsanti anuvicca suve suve
acchiddavuttiṃ medhāviṃ paññāsīlasamāhitaṃ

nekkhaṃ jambonadass'eva ko taṃ ninditum arahati
devā'pi naṃ pasaṃsanti brahmunā'pi pasaṃsito

231

kāyappakopaṃ rakkheyya kāyena saṃvuto siyā
kāyaduccaritaṃ hitvā kāyena sucaritaṃ care

226

The influxes of passion disappear in those who are ever vigilant, who are absorbed day and night in spiritual studies, and who are bent on realization of nirvana.

227

This is an old saying, O Atula, not one merely of today: "They blame him who remains silent, they blame him who speaks much, they even blame him who speaks in moderation." There is none in this world who is not blamed.

228

There never existed, nor will there ever exist, nor does there exist today anyone who is always scorned or always praised.

229, 230

If wise men, after due observation day after day, praise one who is flawless in character, highly intelligent and endowed with religious insight and virtue, who is like unto a coin made of the purest gold from the Jambū river – who would dare censure such a man? Even the devas praise him; he is praised even by Brahmā.

231

One should guard against the agitations of the body; he should be restrained in body. Having abandoned the bodily sins,* he should cultivate good conduct in body.

*Bodily sins are threefold: 1) killing; 2) stealing; 3) adultery.

232

vacīpakopaṃ rakkheyya vācāya saṃvuto siyā
vacīduccaritaṃ hitvā vācāya sucaritaṃ care

233

manopakopaṃ rakkheyya manasā saṃvuto siyā
manoduccaritaṃ hitvā manasā sucaritaṃ care

234

kāyena saṃvutā dhīrā atho vācāya saṃvutā
manasā saṃvutā dhīrā te ve suparisaṃvutā

232

One should guard against the agitations of speech; he should be restrained in speech. Having abandoned the verbal sins,* he should cultivate good conduct in speech.

233

One should guard against the agitations of mind; he should be restrained of mind. Having abandoned the mental sins,† he should cultivate good conduct in mind.

234

The wise who are controlled in body, who likewise are controlled in speech, those wise men who are controlled in mind, are indeed well controlled.

---

*Verbal sins are fourfold: 1) falsehood; 2) slander; 3) obscene speech; 4) idle gossip.

†Mental sins are: 1) covetousness; 2) malevolence; 3) false views.

MALAVAGGO AṬṬHĀRASAMO

235

paṇḍupalāso'va'dāni'si yamapurisā'pi ca taṃ upaṭṭhitā
uyyogamukhe ca tiṭṭhasi pātheyyampi ca te na vijjati

236

so karohi dīpam attano khippaṃ vāyama paṇḍito bhava
niddhantamalo anaṅgaṇo dibbaṃ ariyabhūmim ehisi

237

upanītavayo ca'dāni'si sampayāto'si yamassa santike
vāso'pi ca te n'atthi antarā pātheyyampi ca te na vijjati

238

so karohi dīpam attano khippaṃ vāyama paṇḍito bhava
niddhantamalo anaṅgaṇo na puna jātijaraṃ upehisi

239

anupubbena medhāvī thokathokaṃ khaṇe khaṇe
kammāro rajatass'eva niddhame malam attano

Impurity – CANTO XVIII

235

You are now like a withered leaf; even the messengers of Yama (death) have drawn near you. You stand at the threshold of departure, with no provision for your journey.

236

Make of yourself a light; strive hard, without delay, and be wise; purged of moral impurities and being thus stainless, you will then enter the celestial realm of the Noble Ones.

237

Your life has now come to a close; you have come into the presence of death. There is no halting-place for you on the way, and no provision have you made for your journey.

238

Make of yourself a light; strive hard, without delay, and be wise; purged of moral impurities and being thus stainless, you will not then come again into birth and old age.

239

Little by little, ever and anon, the wise man should remove his moral impurities as a smith blows away the dross of silver.

240

ayasā va malaṃ samuṭṭhitaṃ taduṭṭhāya tam eva khādati
evaṃ atidhonacārinaṃ sakakammāni nayanti duggatiṃ

241

asajjhāyamalā mantā anuṭṭhānamalā gharā
malaṃ vaṇṇassa kosajjaṃ pamādo rakkhato malaṃ

242

mal'itthiyā duccaritaṃ maccheraṃ dadato malaṃ
malā ve pāpakā dhammā asmiṃ loke paramhi ca

243

tato malā malataraṃ avijjā paramaṃ malaṃ
etaṃ malaṃ pahatvāna nimmalā hotha bhikkhavo

244

sujīvaṃ ahirīkena kākasūrena dhaṃsinā
pakkhandinā pagabbhena saṅkiliṭṭhena jīvitaṃ

245

hirīmatā ca dujjīvaṃ niccaṃ sucigavesinā
alīnen'appagabbhena suddhâjīvena passatā

240

As rust arising from iron straightway corrodes the very iron from which it arose, even so the evil deeds of the transgressor lead him to the state of woe.

241

Non-recitation is the rust of the scriptures; non-exertion is the rust of households; sloth is the rust of beauty; negligence is the rust of a watchman.

242

An unchaste life is the blemish of woman; niggardliness is the taint of a benefactor; impurities are indeed evils in this world and in the next.

243

But there is an impurity greater than all impurities – this is ignorance. Rid yourselves of this greatest impurity, O monks, be you free from all impurities.

244

Life is easy for him who is shameless, impudent as a crow-hero (rascal) and a slanderer, a braggart, arrogant and impure in living.

245

But life is difficult for him who is unassuming, constantly seeking that which is pure, disinterested in worldly things, not boastful, who lives in purity and is endowed with insight.

246, 247

yo pāṇam atipāteti musāvādañ ca bhāsati
loke adinnaṃ ādiyati paradārañ ca gacchati
surāmerayapānañ ca yo naro anuyuñjati
idh'evameso lokasmiṃ mūlaṃ khaṇati attano

248

evam bho purisa jānāhi pāpadhammā asaññatā
mā taṃ lobho adhammo ca ciraṃ dukkhāya randhayuṃ

249

dadāti ve yathāsaddhaṃ yathāpasādanaṃ jano
tattha ve maṅku yo hoti paresaṃ pānabhojane
na so divā vā rattiṃ vā samādhiṃ adhigacchati

250

yassa c'etaṃ samucchinnaṃ mūlaghaccaṃ samūhataṃ
sa ve divā vā rattiṃ vā samādhiṃ adhigacchati

251

n'atthi rāgasamo aggi n'atthi dosasamo gaho
n'atthi mohasamaṃ jālaṃ n'atthi taṇhāsamā nadī

252

sudassaṃ vajjaṃ aññesaṃ attano pana duddasaṃ
paresaṃ hi so vajjāni opuṇāti yathābhusaṃ
attano pana chādeti kaliṃ'va kitavā saṭho

246, 247

He who destroys life here, who utters untruth, who takes what is not given to him, who goes to the wife of another, who indulges in intoxicating liquors, such a man, while in this world, destroys the root of his being.

248

Know this, O man, evil-natured ones are unrestrained; let not greed and wrongdoing lead you to untold misery for a long time.

249

People give alms according to their faith and inclination. But he who frets about the drink and food given to others does not attain peace of mind by day or by night.

250

He in whom that feeling is totally uprooted and destroyed, that person attains peace of mind by day and by night.

251

There is no fire like passion; there is no stranglehold like hatred; there is no snare like delusion; there is no torrent like craving.

252

The faults of others are easily seen, but one's own faults are perceived with difficulty. One winnows the faults of others like chaff, but conceals his own faults as a fowler covers his body with twigs and leaves.

253

paravajjânupassissa niccaṃ ujjhānasaññino
āsavā tassa vaḍḍhanti ārā so āsavakkhayā

254

ākāse padaṃ n'atthi samaṇo n'atthi bāhire
papañcâbhiratā pajā nippapañcā tathāgatā

255

ākāse padaṃ n'atthi samaṇo n'atthi bāhire
saṅkhārā sassatā n'atthi n'atthi buddhānam iñjitaṃ

253

If a man sees only the faults of others, and is ever taking offense, his appetite for sense pleasures increases and he is far from the eradication of his desires.

254

There is no footprint in the sky (*ākāsa*); there is no ascetic outwardly. Mankind delights in the illusory world; the Tathāgatas (Buddhas) find no delight therein.

255

There is no footprint in the sky; there is no ascetic outwardly; no composite things are eternal; there is no instability in the Buddhas.

DHAMMAṬṬHAVAGGO EKŪNAVĪSATIMO

256

na tena hoti dhammaṭṭho yen'atthaṃ sahasā naye
yo ca atthaṃ anatthañ ca ubho niccheyya paṇḍito

257

asāhasena dhammena samena nayatī pare
dhammassa gutto medhāvī dhammaṭṭho'ti pavuccati

258

na tena paṇḍito hoti yāvatā bahu bhāsati
khemī averī abhayo paṇḍito'ti pavuccati

259

na tāvatā dhammadharo yāvatā bahu bhāsati
yo ca appampi sutvāna dhammaṃ kāyena passati
sa ve dhammadharo hoti yo dhammaṃ nappamajjati

260

na tena thero hoti yen'assa phalitaṃ siro
paripakko vayo tassa moghajiṇṇo'ti vuccati

The Righteous – Canto XIX

256

He who arbitrates a case by force does not thereby become just (established in Dhamma). But the wise man is he who carefully discriminates between right and wrong.

257

He who leads others by nonviolence, righteously and equitably, is indeed a guardian of justice, wise and righteous.

258

One is not wise merely because he talks much. But he who is calm, free from hatred and fear, is verily called a wise man.

259

One is not a supporter of Dhamma merely because he talks much. But he who hears only a little of the Law, yet perceives its essence by diligent exertion, and does not neglect it, is indeed a true supporter of Dhamma.

260

One does not become an elder by reason of his hair being grey. Of course, he may be ripe in age, but he is a person "grown old in vain."

261

yamhi saccañ ca dhammo ca ahiṃsā saññamo damo
sa ve vantamalo dhīro thero iti pavuccati

262

na vākkaraṇamattena vaṇṇapokkharatāya vā
sādhurūpo naro hoti issukī maccharī saṭho

263

yassa c'etaṃ samucchinnaṃ mūlaghaccaṃ samūhataṃ
sa vantadoso medhāvī sādhurūpo'ti vuccati

264

na muṇḍakena samaṇo abbato alikaṃ bhaṇaṃ
icchālobhasamāpanno samaṇo kiṃ bhavissati

265

yo ca sameti pāpāni aṇuṃ thūlāni sabbaso
samitattā hi pāpānaṃ samaṇo'ti pavuccati

266

na tena bhikkhu so hoti yāvatā bhikkhate pare
vissaṃ dhammaṃ samādāya bhikkhu hoti na tāvatā

267

yo'dha puññañ ca pāpañ ca bāhetvā brahmacariyavā
saṅkhāya loke carati sa ve bhikkhū'ti vuccati

261

He in whom there dwell truth, virtue, nonviolence, self-restraint and moderation, such a wise monk who has cast away all impurities is indeed called an elder (*thera*).

262

Not by mere ornate speech, nor by a beautiful complexion, does a man who is jealous, selfish and crafty become worthy of respect.

263

But he in whom these evils are completely uprooted and extinguished, who has given up hatred and is wise – indeed he is called worthy of respect.

264

Not by tonsure does one who is undisciplined and utters lies become a monk. How can he who is overcome by desire and greed become a monk?

265

But he who constantly stills his evil tendencies, small or great, is called a true monk (*samaṇa*), because he has quieted all these evils.

266

He is not a religious mendicant because he begs alms from others. He does not become a bhikkhu merely by outward observances of the Law.

267

But he who has transcended both merit and demerit, who leads a life of purity and lives in this world in full realization of the Truth, he indeed is called a bhikkhu.

268, 269

na monena munī hoti mūḷharūpo aviddasu
yo ca tulaṃ'va paggayha varam ādāya paṇḍito

pāpāni parivajjeti sa munī tena so munī
yo munāti ubho loke munī tena pavuccati

270

na tena ariyo hoti yena pāṇāni hiṃsati
ahiṃsā sabbapāṇānaṃ ariyo'ti pavuccati

271, 272

na sīlabbatamattena bāhusaccena vā puna
athavā samādhilābhena vivicca sayanena vā

phusāmi nekkhammasukhaṃ aputhujjanasevitaṃ
bhikkhu vissâsamāpādi appatto āsavakkhayaṃ

268, 269

By quietude alone one does not become a sage (*muni*) if he is foolish and ignorant. But he who, as if holding a pair of scales, takes the good and shuns the evil, is a wise man; he is indeed a muni by that very reason. He who understands both good and evil as they really are, is called a true sage.

270

He who injures living beings is not an Ariya (noble). By nonviolence towards all living beings one becomes an Ariya.

271, 272

Not merely by the practice of morality and self-discipline nor by great learning, not even by samādhi (profound spiritual contemplation) or by a life of seclusion, do I reach the bliss of freedom which is not attainable by the ordinary mortal. O bhikkhu, rest not content until you have attained the extinction of all desires.

MAGGAVAGGO VĪSATIMO

273

maggān'aṭṭhaṅgiko seṭṭho saccānaṃ caturo padā
virāgo seṭṭho dhammānaṃ dipadānañ ca cakkhumā

274

eso'va maggo n'atth'añño dassanassa visuddhiyā
etamhi tumhe paṭipajjatha mārass'etaṃ pamohanaṃ

275

etamhi tumhe paṭipannā dukkhass'antaṃ karissatha
akkhāto ve mayā maggo aññāya sallasanthanaṃ

276

tumhehi kiccaṃ ātappaṃ akkhātāro tathāgatā
paṭipannā pamokkhanti jhāyino mārabandhanā

277

sabbe saṅkhārā aniccā ti yadā paññāya passati
atha nibbindatī dukkhe esa maggo visuddhiyā

The Path – Canto XX

273

Of paths the Eightfold is the best; of truths the Four Noble Truths are the best; of all states Detachment is the best; of men* the Seeing One (Buddha) is the foremost.

274

This is the path; there is no other path that leads to purity of insight. Follow this path, for this path bewilders the Evil One (Māra).

275

Having entered upon the path you will come to an end of your suffering. Having myself recognized this, I proclaimed this path which removes all thorns.

276

You yourself must make the effort. The Tathāgatas (Buddhas) can only point the way. Those who have entered the path and become meditative are freed from the fetters of Māra.

277

"Transient are all composite things"; he who perceives the truth of this gets disgusted with this world of suffering. This is the path to purity.

**Dipadāna* (from *dvi* + *pada*), "bipeds" (men).

278

sabbe saṅkhārā dukkhā ti yadā paññāya passati
atha nibbindatī dukkhe esa maggo visuddhiyā

279

sabbe dhammā anattā ti yadā paññāya passati
atha nibbindatī dukkhe esa maggo visuddhiyā

280

uṭṭhānakālamhi anuṭṭhahāno
yuvā balī ālasiyaṃ upeto
saṃsannasaṅkappamano kusīto
paññāya maggaṃ alaso na vindati

281

vācānurakkhī manasā susaṃvuto
kāyena ca akusalaṃ na kayirā
ete tayo kammapathe visodhaye
ārādhaye maggam isippaveditaṃ

282

yogā ve jāyatī bhūri ayogā bhūri saṅkhayo
etaṃ dvedhāpathaṃ ñatvā bhavāya vibhavāya ca
tath'attānaṃ niveseyya yathā bhūri pavaḍḍhati

283

vanaṃ chindatha mā rukkhaṃ vanato jāyatī bhayaṃ
chetvā vanañ ca vanathañ ca nibbanā hotha bhikkhavo

278

"Sorrowful are all composite things"; he who perceives the truth of this gets disgusted with this world of suffering. This is the path to purity.

279

"All forms of existence are unreal" (*an-attā*); he who perceives the truth of this gets disgusted with this world of suffering. This is the path to purity.

280

He who does not get up when it is time to do so; who, although youthful and strong, is yet given to indolence, is weak in resolution and thought – such an idle and lazy person does not find the path to wisdom.

281

One should be watchful over his speech, well-restrained in mind, and commit no unwholesome deed with his body. Let him purify this threefold avenue of action (karma), and he will tread the path made known by the sages.

282

Verily, from devotion (*yoga*) arises wisdom, from non-devotion springs the loss of wisdom. Having become aware of this twofold path that leads to progress and decline, let him place himself in such a way that his wisdom increases.

283

Cut down the whole forest (of desires), not just a tree. From the forest arises fear. Cut down the forest and its brushwood, O monks, and be emancipated.

284

yāvaṃ (hi) vanatho na chijjati aṇumatto'pi narassa nārisu
paṭibaddhamano'va tāva so vaccho khīrapako'va mātari

285

ucchinda sineham attano kumudaṃ sāradikaṃ'va pāṇinā
santimaggam eva brūhaya nibbānaṃ sugatena desitaṃ

286

idha vassaṃ vasissāmi idha hemantagimhisu
iti bālo vicinteti antarāyaṃ na bujjhati

287

taṃ puttapasusammattaṃ byāsattamanasaṃ naraṃ
suttaṃ gāmaṃ mahogho'va maccu ādāya gacchati

288

na santi puttā tāṇāya na pitā n'āpi bandhavā
antakenādhipannassa n'atthi ñātīsu tāṇatā

289

etam atthavasaṃ ñatvā paṇḍito sīlasaṃvuto
nibbānagamanaṃ maggaṃ khippam eva visodhaye

284

As long as the brushwood of a man's lust towards women is not completely destroyed, even to the last seedling, so long is his mind fettered as a suckling calf is bound to its mother.

285

Cut off the love of self as one would pluck an autumnal white lotus. Proceed then upon that (Eightfold) path of peace – the nirvana as expounded by Sugata (Buddha).

286

"Here shall I dwell in the rainy season; here shall I dwell in winter and summer." Thus the fool muses, but never reflects on the dangers that might befall him.

287

As a great flood carries off a sleeping village, so death seizes and carries off a man who is distracted and overly attached to his children and cattle.

288

Sons are no protection, neither father nor kinsfolk; when one is assailed by death, there is no protection among one's kin.

289

Having perceived this significant fact, let the wise and self-restrained man quickly clear the path that leads to nirvana.

PAKIṆṆAKAVAGGO EKAVĪSATIMO

290

mattāsukhapariccāgā passe ce vipulaṃ sukhaṃ
caje mattāsukhaṃ dhīro sampassaṃ vipulaṃ sukhaṃ

291

paradukkhūpadhānena yo attano sukham icchati
verasaṃsaggasaṃsaṭṭho verā so na pamuccati

292

yaṃ hi kiccaṃ tad'apaviddhaṃ akiccaṃ pana kayirati
unnaḷānaṃ pamattānaṃ tesaṃ vaḍḍhanti āsavā

293

yesañ ca susamāraddhā niccaṃ kāyagatā sati
akiccaṃ te na sevanti kicce sātaccakārino
satānaṃ sampajānānaṃ atthaṃ gacchanti āsavā

294

mātaraṃ pitaraṃ hantvā rājāno dve ca khattiye
raṭṭhaṃ sānucaraṃ hantvā anīgho yāti brāhmaṇo

Miscellaneous Verses – CANTO XXI

290

If by renouncing a small pleasure one derives great bliss, the wise man relinquishes that smaller pleasure in view of the greater one.

291

He who desires happiness for himself by inflicting injury on others, is not freed from hatred, being entangled himself in the bonds of hatred.

292

If what ought to be done is neglected, and what ought not to be done is done, then the sensuous influxes of the arrogant and the heedless increase.

293

Those who are constantly watchful as to the nature of the body, who abstain from doing what ought not to be done, who strive to perform the deeds that ought to be done, who are mindful and self-restrained – in such men the sensuous influxes are extinguished.

294

Having slain mother (craving), father (egotism), and the two kings of the Kshatriya caste (the two false doctrines of eternalism and annihilation of the soul), and having destroyed the kingdom with its inhabitants (the twelve bases

295

mātaraṃ pitaraṃ hantvā rājāno dve ca sotthiye
veyyagghapañcamaṃ hantvā anīgho yāti brāhmaṇo

296

suppabuddhaṃ pabujjhanti sadā gotamasāvakā
yesaṃ divā ca ratto ca niccaṃ buddhagatā sati

297

suppabuddhaṃ pabujjhanti sadā gotamasāvakā
yesaṃ divā ca ratto ca niccaṃ dhammagatā sati

298

suppabuddhaṃ pabujjhanti sadā gotamasāvakā
yesaṃ divā ca ratto ca niccaṃ saṅghagatā sati

299

suppabuddhaṃ pabujjhanti sadā gotamasāvakā
yesaṃ divā ca ratto ca niccaṃ kāyagatā sati

300

suppabuddhaṃ pabujjhanti sadā gotamasāvakā
yesaṃ divā ca ratto ca ahiṃsāya rato mano

of sense perception and objects of attachment), the true Brāhman goes his way unperturbed.

295

Having slain mother, father and two kings of the Brāhman caste, and having destroyed as the fifth, the tiger (the perilous path of the five hindrances, namely, lust, ill will, torpor, restlessness and doubt), the true Brāhman goes his way unperturbed.

296

The disciples of Gotama (Gautama) always awake well-enlightened. Their consciousness is constantly centered, day and night, on the Buddha.

297

The disciples of Gotama always awake well-enlightened. Their consciousness is constantly centered, day and night, on the Dhamma.

298

The disciples of Gotama always awake well-enlightened. Their consciousness is constantly centered, day and night, on the Order (*saṅgha*).

299

The disciples of Gotama always awake well-enlightened. Their consciousness is constantly centered, day and night, upon (the transitory nature of) the body.

300

The disciples of Gotama always awake well-enlightened. Their consciousness, by day and night, delights in the virtue of nonviolence (*ahiṃsā*).

301

suppabuddhaṃ pabujjhanti sadā gotamasāvakā
yesaṃ divā ca ratto ca bhāvanāya rato mano

302

duppabbajjaṃ durabhiramaṃ durāvāsā gharā dukhā
dukkho'samānasaṃvāso dukkhānupatit'addhagū
tasmā na c'addhagū siyā na ca dukkhānupatito siyā

303

saddho sīlena sampanno yasobhogasamappito
yaṃ yaṃ padesaṃ bhajati tattha tatth'eva pūjito

304

dūre santo pakāsenti himavanto'va pabbato
asant'ettha na dissanti ratti khittā yathā sarā

305

ekāsanaṃ ekaseyyaṃ eko caram atandito
eko damayam attānaṃ vanante ramito siyā

301

The disciples of Gotama always awake well-enlightened. Their consciousness, by day and night, delights in contemplation.

302

Renunciation of the worldly life is difficult; difficult is it to be happy in the monastic life; equally difficult and painful is it to lead a householder's life. Association with the unsympathetic is also painful. Woe befalls the wayfarer (who enters the cycle of births and deaths). Therefore be not a traveler (in *saṃsāra*); fall not a victim of sorrow!

303

He who is endowed with devotion and virtue and is blessed with fame and wealth, is revered wherever he goes.

304

Good men shine from afar like the snowy peaks of the Himalayas. But the wicked, like arrows shot in the night, are not seen.

305

Sitting alone, sleeping alone, living alone, and being diligent, subduing the self by means of the Self, let a man find delight in the ending of the forest (of desires).

NIRAYAVAGGO DVĀVĪSATIMO

306

abhūtavādī nirayaṃ upeti yo cā'pi katvā na karomi c'āha
ubho'pi te pecca samā bhavanti nihīnakammā manujā parattha

307

kāsāvakaṇṭhā bahavo pāpadhammā asaññatā
pāpā pāpehi kammehi nirayaṃ te upapajjare

308

seyyo ayoguḷo bhutto tatto aggisikhūpamo
yañ ce bhuñjeyya dussīlo raṭṭhapiṇḍaṃ asaññato

309

cattāri ṭhānāni naro pamatto āpajjatī paradārûpasevī
apuññalābhaṃ na nikāmaseyyaṃ nindaṃ tatiyaṃ nirayaṃ catutthaṃ

310

apuññalābho ca gatī ca pāpikā bhītassa bhītāya ratī ca thokikā
rājā ca daṇḍaṃ garukaṃ paṇeti tasmā naro paradāraṃ na seve

The Woeful State – Canto XXII

306

The man who utters a falsehood goes to the woeful state (hell), as does he who having committed an act says, "I did not commit it." After death both these men of contemptible deeds become equal in the next world.

307

Many of those who wear the saffron robe are of evil character and unrestrained. These evildoers are born in hell by reason of their sinful deeds.

308

It is far better for an irreligious and unrestrained monk to swallow a flaming ball of red-hot iron than to feed on the alms of the people.

309

Four wretched conditions befall the heedless man who commits adultery: demerit, broken sleep, scorn as third, and birth in hell as fourth.

310

There is the acquirement of demerit as well as of rebirth in an evil state; even the fleeting pleasure of the man in the arms of the woman is accompanied by fear; and, moreover, the penalty inflicted by the Rājā is heavy. Therefore, a man should not commit adultery.

311

kuso yathā duggahito hattham evânukantati
sāmaññaṃ dupparāmaṭṭhaṃ nirayāy'ūpakaḍḍhati

312

yaṃ kiñci sithilaṃ kammaṃ saṅkiliṭṭhañ ca yaṃ vataṃ
saṅkassaraṃ brahmacariyaṃ na taṃ hoti mahapphalaṃ

313

kayirā ce kayirāth'etaṃ daḷham enaṃ parakkame
saṭhilohi paribbājo bhiyyo ākirate rajaṃ

314

akataṃ dukkataṃ seyyo pacchā tapati dukkataṃ
katañ ca sukataṃ seyyo yaṃ katvā nânutappati

315

nagaraṃ yathā paccantaṃ guttaṃ santarabāhiraṃ
evaṃ gopetha attānaṃ khaṇo ve mā upaccagā
khaṇâtītā hi socanti nirayamhi samappitā

316

alajjitāye lajjanti lajjitāye na lajjare
micchādiṭṭhisamādānā sattā gacchanti duggatiṃ

317

abhaye ca bhayadassino bhaye câbhayadassino
micchādiṭṭhisamādānā sattā gacchanti duggatiṃ

311

Just as a blade of kuśa grass when wrongly handled cuts the hand, so does asceticism when wrongly practiced drag one to the woeful state.

312

Any act performed halfheartedly, any religious rite observed improperly, or continence reluctantly practiced – none of these produces great fruit.

313

If anything ought to be done, let a man perform that deed with all his might; an ascetic who is lax scatters more and more dust (of passion).

314

An evil act is better left undone, for that evil deed causes torment afterwards. It is better to perform a good deed; by performing it one does not repent later.

315

As a frontier city, well-guarded within and without, so guard yourself. Do not lose a single moment, for those who let opportunity slip away do indeed grieve when they are born in the woeful state (hell).

316

Those who are ashamed of what they ought not to be ashamed of, and are not ashamed of what they ought to be, such men, embracing erroneous views, enter the woeful path.

317

Those who are fearful when there is no cause for fear, and feel no fear when they should, such men, embracing erroneous views, enter the woeful path.

318

avajje vajjamatino vajje câvajjadassino
micchādiṭṭhisamādānā sattā gacchanti duggatiṃ

319

vajjañ ca vajjato ñatvā avajjañ ca avajjato
sammādiṭṭhisamādānā sattā gacchanti suggatiṃ

318

Those who imagine error where there is none, and do not see it where it does exist, such men, embracing false views, enter the woeful path.

319

Those who discern error as error and truth as truth, such men, embracing right views, enter the path of bliss.

NĀGAVAGGO TEVĪSATIMO

320

ahaṃ nāgo'va saṅgāme cāpāto patitaṃ saraṃ
ativākyaṃ titikkhissaṃ dussīlo hi bahujjano

321

dantaṃ nayanti samitiṃ dantaṃ rājâbhirūhati
danto seṭṭho manussesu yo'tivākyaṃ titikkhati

322

varam assatarā dantā ājānīyā ca sindhavā
kuñjarā ca mahānāgā attadanto tato varaṃ

323

na hi etehi yānehi gaccheyya agataṃ disaṃ
yathā'ttanā sudantena danto dantena gacchati

324

dhanapālako nāma kuñjaro
kaṭukappabhedano dunnivārayo
baddho kabalaṃ na bhuñjati
sumarati nāgavanassa kuñjaro

The Elephant – CANTO XXIII

320

Even as an elephant on the battlefield endures the arrow shot from the bow, so shall I bear with abusive language. Verily, most people are ill-tempered.

321

They lead a well-trained elephant to the assembly; the king mounts a well-tamed elephant. The self-controlled man who can bear with abusive language is the best among men.

322

When trained, mules are good, so also are the horses of Sindhu breed and the great tuskers of noble lineage. But better than all these is the man who has controlled the senses.

323

Not astride any of these (animals) can one reach the untrodden realm (nirvana), where a well-disciplined man goes only on his well-tamed (nature), his well-controlled self.

324

The royal tusker named Dhanapālaka, with sap-flowing temples in its rut period, is difficult to control. It does not eat a morsel when bound. It eagerly longs for the elephant forest.

325

middhī yadā hoti mahagghaso ca
niddāyitā samparivattasāyī
mahāvarāho'va nivāpapuṭṭho
punappunaṃ gabbham upeti mando

326

idaṃ pure cittam acāri cārikaṃ
yenicchakaṃ yatthakāmaṃ yathāsukhaṃ
tadajj'ahaṃ niggahessāmi yoniso
hatthippabhinnaṃ viya aṅkusaggaho

327

appamādaratā hotha sacittam anurakkhatha
duggā uddharath'attānaṃ paṅke satto'va kuñjaro

328

sace labhetha nipakaṃ sahāyaṃ
saddhiṃ caraṃ sādhuvihāridhīraṃ
abhibhuyya sabbāni parissayāni
careyya ten'attamano satīmā

329

no ce labhetha nipakaṃ sahāyaṃ
saddhiṃ caraṃ sādhuvihāridhīraṃ
rājā'va raṭṭhaṃ vijitaṃ pahāya
eko care mātaṅg'araññe'va nāgo

330

ekassa caritaṃ seyyo n'atthi bāle sahāyatā
eko care na ca pāpāni kayirā appossukko mātaṅg'araññe'va nāgo

325

If a man is torpid, gluttonous, slumberous and rolling to and fro like a huge hog which has been fattened by pig wash and podder, that indolent and stupid fool is born again and again.

326

During the past, this mind of mine roamed freely as it liked, as it desired, at its own pleasure. But today, I shall fully keep it in check, even as the elephant driver with the point of a goad controls an unruly elephant in rut.

327

Be ever vigilant; keep close watch over your thoughts; extricate yourself from the mire of evil, as does an elephant sunk in the mud.

328

If you find a wise companion to associate with you, one who leads a virtuous life and is diligent, you should lead a life with him joyfully and mindfully, conquering all obstacles.

329

If you do not find a wise companion to associate with you, one who leads a virtuous life and is diligent, then like the monarch who has renounced his conquered kingdom, and like Mātanga the elephant in the forest, you should live alone.

330

It is better to lead a solitary life; there is no companionship with a childish person! Let one live alone committing no sin, having few wishes, like Mātanga the elephant in the elephant grove.

331

atthamhi jātamhi sukhā sahāyā
tuṭṭhī sukhā yā itarītarena
puññaṃ sukhaṃ jīvitasaṅkhayamhi
sabbassa dukkhassa sukhaṃ pahānaṃ

332

sukhā matteyyatā loke atho petteyyatā sukhā
sukhā sāmaññatā loke atho brahmaññatā sukhā

333

sukhaṃ yāva jarā sīlaṃ sukhā saddhā patiṭṭhitā
sukho paññāya paṭilābho pāpānaṃ akaraṇaṃ sukhaṃ

331

Companions are pleasant to have when a need arises; contentment is pleasant when it is mutual; merit is pleasant at the last hour; pleasant is the extinction of all suffering.

332

To be a mother in this world is bliss; to be a father in this world is bliss; to be a homeless recluse in this world is bliss, and to be a Brāhman in this world is bliss (*sukha*).

This stanza may also be translated as follows:

To render service unto a mother in this world is bliss; to render service unto a father in this world is bliss; to render service unto a homeless recluse in this world is bliss, and to render service unto a Brāhman sage in this world is bliss.

333

The virtue that lasts to the end of life is bliss; steadfast faith is also bliss; the attainment of wisdom is bliss, and not to commit sin is bliss.

TAṆHĀVAGGO CATUVĪSATIMO

334

manujassa pamattacārino
taṇhā vaḍḍhati māluvā viya
so plavati hurāhuraṃ
phalam icchaṃ va vanamhi vānaro

335

yaṃ esā sahatī jammī taṇhā loke visattikā
sokā tassa pavaḍḍhanti abhivaṭṭaṃ va bīraṇaṃ

336

yo c'etaṃ sahatī jammiṃ taṇhaṃ loke duraccayaṃ
sokā tamhā papatanti udabindū'va pokkharā

337

taṃ vo vadāmi bhaddaṃ vo yāvant'ettha samāgatā
taṇhāya mūlaṃ khaṇatha usīrattho'va bīraṇaṃ
mā vo naḷaṃ va soto'va māro bhañji punappunaṃ

338

yathā'pi mūle anupaddave daḷhe
chinno'pi rukkho punar eva rūhati

Thirst or Craving – CANTO XXIV

334

The craving (*taṇhā*) of a heedless man grows like the māluvā creeper. He jumps (from life to life) like a monkey eagerly seeking fruit in the forest.

335

Whosoever is overcome by this shameful craving which creates entanglements in this world, his sorrows increase like the luxuriant bīrana grass (in the rainy season).

336

But whosoever overcomes in this world this shameful craving, which is difficult to suppress, finds his sorrows fall from him, as drops of water from a lotus leaf.

337

This I say unto you! May all of you, who are gathered here, be blessed! May you dig up the root of craving as one who digs up the bīrana grass for the fragrant usīra root.* Let not Māra destroy you again and again, even as the current of the river destroys the reeds.

338

Just as a tree when cut down sprouts up again if the roots remain firm and uninjured, even so this suffering (of

*Andropogon Muricatus, cuscus grass.

evampi taṇhānusaye anūhate
nibbattatī dukkhamidaṃ punappunaṃ

339

yassa chattiṃsatī sotā manāpassavanā bhusā
vāhā vahanti duddiṭṭhiṃ saṅkappā rāganissitā

340

savanti sabbadhī sotā latā ubbhijja tiṭṭhati
tañ ca disvā lataṃ jātaṃ mūlaṃ paññāya chindatha

341

saritāni sinehitāni ca
somanassāni bhavanti jantuno
te sātasitā sukhesino
te ve jātijarūpagā narā

342

tasiṇāya purakkhatā pajā
parisappanti saso'va bādhito
saṃyojanasaṅgasattā
dukkhamupenti punappunaṃ cirāya

343

tasiṇāya purakkhatā pajā
parisappanti saso'va bādhito
tasmā tasiṇaṃ vinodaye
bhikkhu ākaṅkhī virāgam attano

344

yo nibbanatho vanâdhimutto
vanamutto vanam eva dhāvati

life) returns again and again if the root of craving is not completely destroyed.

339

The man in whom the thirty-six streams of craving flow strongly towards pleasurable objects, the waves of passions carry off. He is of confused vision and erroneous thoughts.

340

Streams flow everywhere; the creeper (of passion) sprouts and remains fixed. If you see that creeper springing up, cut its root by means of wisdom.

341

In creatures there arise pleasures extending towards sense objects. Immersed in various enjoyments they hanker after them. Verily, these people are subject to birth and old age.

342

People beset by craving circle round and round, like a hare ensnared in a net; held fast by the (ten) fetters and shackles (that bind man to the wheel of life), they undergo suffering for a long time, again and again.

343

People beset by craving circle round and round, like a hare ensnared in a net; therefore, let the monk who desires freedom from passion abandon craving.

344

He who has renounced the forest (of craving), and having liberated himself from that forest, yet runs back into

taṃ puggalam eva passatha
mutto bandhanam eva dhāvati

345

na taṃ daḷhaṃ bandhanam āhu dhīrā
yadāyasaṃ dārujaṃ babbajañ ca
sārattarattā maṇikuṇḍalesu
puttesu dāresu ca yā apekhā

346

etaṃ daḷhaṃ bandhanam āhu dhīrā
ohārinaṃ sithilaṃ duppamuñcaṃ
etampi chetvāna paribbajanti
anapekkhino kāmasukhaṃ pahāya

347

ye rāgarattānupatanti sotaṃ
sayaṃ kataṃ makkaṭako'va jālaṃ
etampi chetvāna vajanti dhīrā
anapekkhino sabbadukkhaṃ pahāya

348

muñca pure, muñca pacchato
majjhe muñca bhavassa pāragū
sabbattha vimuttamānaso
na puna jātijaraṃ upehisi

349

vitakkapamathitassa jantuno tibbarāgassa subhānupassino
bhiyyo taṇhā pavaḍḍhati esa kho daḷhaṃ karoti bandhanaṃ

it — behold this man! Although once freed, he runs into bondage.

345

The wise do not call strong that fetter which is made of iron, wood or hemp. Rather do they call attachment to jewels, ornaments, children and wives a far stronger fetter.

346

That fetter is strong, say the wise, which drags a man down; which, although slack, is difficult to escape from. Severing even this, they set forth, desiring nothing and abandoning all sensuous pleasures.

347

Those beings who are infatuated with the fire of lust fall into the current (of thirst for life), as the spider into its self-spun web. The wise, having curtailed the current, go off, leaving all sorrow behind.

348

Renounce the craving for the past, renounce the craving for the future, renounce the craving for what is between, and cross to the opposite shore. With the mind fully emancipated you will not return to birth and old age.

349

Craving (*taṇhā*) steadily grows in the mortal whose mind is agitated by (evil) thoughts, who is full of strong passions and ever yearning for what is pleasant. Such a one makes his fetters strong.

350

vitakkûpasame ca yo rato
asubhaṃ bhāvayatī sadā sato
esa kho vyantikāhiti
esa checchati mārabandhanaṃ

351

niṭṭhaṅgato asantāsī vītataṇho anaṅgaṇo
acchindi bhavasallāni antimo'yaṃ samussayo

352

vītataṇho anādāno niruttipadakovido
akkharānaṃ sannipātaṃ jaññā pubbāparāni ca
sa ve antimasārīro mahāpañño mahāpuriso ti vuccati

353

sabbâbhibhū sabbavidū'hamasmi
sabbesu dhammesu anūpalitto
sabbañjaho taṇhakkhaye vimutto
sayaṃ abhiññāya kamuddiseyyaṃ

354

sabbadānaṃ dhammadānaṃ jināti
sabbaṃ rasaṃ dhammaraso jināti
sabbaṃ ratiṃ dhammaratī jināti
taṇhakkhayo sabbadukkhaṃ jināti

355

hananti bhogā dummedhaṃ no ce pāragavesino
bhogataṇhāya dummedho hanti aññe'va attanaṃ

350

He who delights in controlling his thoughts, who ever absorbs himself in contemplation on what is not pleasant (the impurity of the body), such a one will put an end (to craving) and cut the bonds of Māra.

351

He who has arrived at the goal, who is fearless, devoid of craving, passionless, has destroyed the arrows of existence. For such a person this is his last physical form.

352

He who is devoid of craving and attachment, who is an expert in etymology and terminology, who knows the systematic arrangement of letters (in their prior and posterior relations), is called a foremost sage, a great man. He bears a physical body for the last time.

353

"I am the conqueror of all, I am the knower of all, in all the states of life. I am unattached, I have relinquished all, and with the destruction of craving I am liberated. Having comprehended everything by myself, whom shall I call my teacher?"

354

The gift of Truth (*dhamma*) excels all other gifts; the flavor of Truth excels all other flavors; the delight in Truth surpasses all delights. The destruction of craving overcomes all suffering.

355

Riches destroy the ignorant, yet not those who seek the further shore. Through his craving for material wealth, he destroys himself as if (destroying) others.

356

tiṇadosāni khettāni rāgadosā ayaṃ pajā
tasmā hi vītarāgesu dinnaṃ hoti mahapphalaṃ

357

tiṇadosāni khettāni dosadosā ayaṃ pajā
tasmā hi vītadosesu dinnaṃ hoti mahapphalaṃ

358

tiṇadosāni khettāni mohadosā ayaṃ pajā
tasmā hi vītamohesu dinnaṃ hoti mahapphalaṃ

359

tiṇadosāni khettāni icchādosā ayaṃ pajā
tasmā hi vigaticchesu dinnaṃ hoti mahapphalaṃ

356

Fields have the blight of weeds; mankind has the blight of passion; therefore, offerings given to those devoid of passion bring forth abundant fruit.

357

Fields have the blight of weeds; mankind has the blight of hatred; therefore, offerings given to those devoid of hatred bring forth abundant fruit.

358

Fields have the blight of weeds; mankind has the blight of delusion; therefore, offerings given to those devoid of delusion bring forth abundant fruit.

359

Fields have the blight of weeds; mankind has the blight of desire; therefore, offerings given to those devoid of desire bring forth abundant fruit.

BHIKKHUVAGGO PAÑCAVĪSATIMO

360

cakkhunā saṃvaro sādhu sādhu sotena saṃvaro
ghāṇena saṃvaro sādhu sādhu jivhāya saṃvaro

361

kāyena saṃvaro sādhu sādhu vācāya saṃvaro
manasā saṃvaro sādhu sādhu sabbattha saṃvaro
sabbattha saṃvuto bhikkhu sabbadukkhā pamuccati

362

hatthasaññato pādasaññato vācāya saññato saññatuttamo
ajjhattarato samāhito eko santusito tamāhu bhikkhuṃ

363

yo mukhasaññato bhikkhu mantabhāṇī anuddhato
atthaṃ dhammañ ca dīpeti madhuraṃ tassa bhāsitaṃ

364

dhammārāmo dhammarato dhammaṃ anuvicintayaṃ
dhammaṃ anussaraṃ bhikkhu saddhammā na parihāyati

The Mendicant – CANTO XXV

360

Restraint through the eye is good; good is restraint through the ear; restraint through the nose is good and good is restraint through the tongue.

361

Restraint in body is good and good is restraint in speech; restraint by the mind is good and good is restraint in all things. The mendicant who is restrained in every respect is liberated from all suffering.

362

He who is controlled in hand, foot, and in speech, who is well disciplined and practices the utmost restraint; he who delights inwardly, in concentration, who leads a solitary life and is content – him they call a bhikkhu (mendicant).

363

The mendicant who restrains his tongue, who speaks with wisdom, who is not conceited, who illuminates the inner meaning (and letter) of the Law (*dhamma*), sweet indeed is his utterance.

364

The mendicant who dwells in the Law, who glories in the Law, who meditates on the Law, who ever follows the Law, does not fall away from the true Dhamma.

365

salābhaṃ nâtimaññeyya nâññesaṃ pihayaṃ care
aññesaṃ pihayaṃ bhikkhu samādhiṃ nâdhigacchati

366

appalābho'pi ce bhikkhu salābhaṃ nâtimaññati
taṃ ve devā pasaṃsanti suddhâjīviṃ atanditaṃ

367

sabbaso nāmarūpasmiṃ yassa n'atthi mamāyitaṃ
asatā ca na socati sa ve bhikkhū'ti vuccati

368

metta vihārī yo bhikkhu pasanno buddhasāsane
adhigacche padaṃ santaṃ saṅkhārûpasamaṃ sukhaṃ

369

siñca bhikkhu imaṃ nāvaṃ sittā te lahumessati
chetvā rāgañ ca dosañ ca tato nibbānam ehisi

370

pañca chinde pañca jahe pañca cuttari bhāvaye
pañca saṅgātigo bhikkhu oghatiṇṇo'ti vuccati

Note — The five fetters that one should cut off are: self-illusion, doubt, clinging to mere rules and rituals, sensuous craving, and ill will.

The five fetters to be renounced are: craving for material existence, craving for immaterial existence, conceit, restlessness, and ignorance.

365

Let the mendicant not underestimate the gift he has received; let him not feel envy for others. The mendicant who envies others does not attain tranquillity of mind.

366

Even the gods praise that mendicant who does not underestimate what he has received, however little, if he is pure and energetic in his life.

367

He who has not any attachment to name and form (mind and body), and does not grieve for what does not really exist – he, indeed, is called a real bhikkhu.

368

The mendicant who lives compassionately, who takes delight in the doctrine of the Enlightened One, will attain that exalted state of peace and happiness, which is the cessation of conditioned existence.

369

Empty this boat, O monk! When emptied, it will go lightly. Cutting off lust and hatred, you will reach nirvana.

370

(Of the fetters) cut off the five, renounce the five, and (of the virtues) cultivate the five. He who has gone beyond the five attachments is called a bhikkhu who has crossed the stream.

To destroy the fetters, the vigilant monk has to cultivate the five virtues: faith, mindfulness, energy, concentration, and wisdom.

The five attachments are: lust, hatred, delusion, pride, and false views.

371

jhāya bhikkhu mā ca pamādo
mā te kāmaguṇe bhamassu cittaṃ
mā lohaguḷaṃ giḷī pamatto
mā kandi dukkham idanti ḍayhamāno

372

n'atthi jhānaṃ apaññassa paññā n'atthi ajjhāyato
yamhi jhānañ ca paññā ca sa ve nibbāna santike

373

suññāgāraṃ paviṭṭhassa santacittassa bhikkhuno
amānusī ratī hoti sammā dhammaṃ vipassato

374

yato yato sammasati khandhānaṃ udayabbayaṃ
labhati pītipāmojjaṃ amataṃ taṃ vijānataṃ

375

tatrāyamādi bhavati idha paññassa bhikkhuno
indriyagutti santuṭṭhī pāṭimokkhe ca saṃvaro
mitte bhajassu kalyāṇe suddhâjīve atandite

371

Meditate, O monk! Be not heedless! Let not your mind wander among the pleasures of the senses, lest through your heedlessness you swallow the red-hot iron ball (in hell) and cry out, as you thus burn – "This is suffering."

372

There is no perfect contemplation for him who is not wise, and no wisdom for him who does not concentrate. He in whom there is both perfect contemplation and wisdom is, indeed, close to nirvana.

373

The mendicant who has withdrawn to a lonely spot, whose heart and mind are tranquil, who clearly perceives the Dhamma, his bliss (of contemplation) is more than human.

374

Whenever one clearly comprehends the origin and destruction of the five aggregates (*khandha*), he experiences bliss and happiness.* This is as the nectar (of immortality) to those who truly comprehend it.

375

In this world this becomes the first requisite for a wise monk: control of the senses, contentment, restraint according to the fundamental code of monastic law; cultivation of noble friends whose lives are pure and who are not indolent.

---

*The five aggregates (Skt. *skandhas*) are: 1) bodily form; 2) feeling; 3) perception; 4) mental formations; 5) consciousness. (See verse 202.)

376

paṭisanthāravuttyassa ācārakusalo siyā
tato pāmojjabahulo dukkhassantaṃ karissasi

377

vassikā viya pupphāni maddavāni pamuñcati
evaṃ rāgañ ca dosañ ca vippamuñcetha bhikkhavo

378

santakāyo santavāco santavā susamāhito
vantalokāmiso bhikkhu upasanto'ti vuccati

379

attanā codayattānaṃ paṭimāse attam attanā
so attagutto satimā sukhaṃ bhikkhu vihāhisi

380

attā hi attano nātho attā hi attano gati
tasmā saññamaya'ttānaṃ assaṃ bhadraṃ'va vāṇijo

381

pāmojjabahulo bhikkhu pasanno buddhasāsane
adhigacche padaṃ santaṃ saṅkhārûpasamaṃ sukhaṃ

382

yo have daharo bhikkhu yuñjati buddhasāsane
so imaṃ lokaṃ pabhāseti abbhā mutto'va candimā

376

The mendicant who is hospitable and friendly, who really lives his ethics and is full of spiritual joy, thereby makes an end of his suffering.

377

Just as the jasmine sheds its withered flowers, even so, O mendicants, you should cast off passion and hatred.

378

That mendicant is called truly tranquil, who is calm in body, calm in speech, calm in mind, who is well-regulated in thoughts and has renounced all worldly allurements.

379

Rouse the self by the Self, restrain the self by the Self, self-guarded and mindful, O monk, you shall live happily.

380

For Self is indeed the protector of oneself; Self is indeed one's destiny. Therefore, curb yourself even as a wise merchant curbs a noble steed.

381

The mendicant who is full of spiritual delight and faith in the doctrine of the Enlightened One will attain the peaceful state (nirvana), the cessation of conditioned existence.

382

The mendicant, though young in years, who applies himself to the teaching of the Awakened One (Gotama), illumines the world, even as the moon when freed from the cloud.

BRĀHMAṆAVAGGO CHAVĪSATIMO

383

chinda sotaṃ parakkamma kāme panuda brāhmaṇa
saṅkhārānaṃ khayaṃ ñatvā akataññū'si brāhmaṇa

384

yadā dvayesu dhammesu pāragū hoti brāhmaṇo
ath'assa sabbe saṃyogā atthaṃ gacchanti jānato

385

yassa pāraṃ apāraṃ vā pārâpāraṃ na vijjati
vītaddaraṃ visaṃyuttaṃ tam ahaṃ brūmi brāhmaṇaṃ

386

jhāyiṃ virajam āsīnaṃ katakiccam anāsavaṃ
uttamatthaṃ anuppattaṃ tam ahaṃ brūmi brāhmaṇaṃ

387

divā tapati ādicco rattiṃ ābhāti candimā
sannaddho khattiyo tapati jhāyī tapati brāhmaṇo
atha sabbamahorattim buddho tapati tejasā

Who is a Brāhman? – Canto XXVI

383

Cut off the stream of craving. Strive hard and renounce the sense pleasures, O Brāhman. When you comprehend the secret of the destruction of all composite things, O Brāhman, you will know the Uncreated (nirvana).

384

When the Brāhman has reached the farther shore of the two states (of tranquillity and insight), then all the fetters of that knowing one disappear.

385

He for whom there exist neither the farther (the external six senses), nor the hither (the internal six senses), nor both of these, and who is devoid of fear and free from fetters – him I call a Brāhman.

386

He who is contemplative, lives without passions, is steadfast and has performed his duties, who is free from sensuous influxes and has attained the highest goal – him I call a Brāhman.

387

The sun shines by day, the moon by night; the warrior is resplendent in armor and the Brāhman radiant in meditation. But Buddha, the Awakened One, illumines both day and night by the splendor of his wisdom.

388

bāhitapāpo'ti brāhmaṇo samacariyā samaṇo'ti vuccati
pabbājayamattano malaṃ tasmā pabbajito'ti vuccati

389

na brāhmaṇassa pahareyya nâssa muñcetha brāhmaṇo
dhī brāhmaṇassa hantāraṃ tato dhī yassa muñcati

390

na brāhmaṇass'etadakiñci seyyo
yadā nisedho manaso piyehi
yato yato hiṃsamano nivattati
tato tato sammati meva dukkhaṃ

391

yassa kāyena vācāya manasā n'atthi dukkataṃ
saṃvutaṃ tīhi ṭhānehi tam ahaṃ brūmi brāhmaṇaṃ

392

yamhā dhammaṃ vijāneyya
sammāsambuddhadesitaṃ
sakkaccaṃ taṃ namasseyya
aggihuttaṃ va brāhmaṇo

393

na jaṭāhi na gottena na jaccā hoti brāhmaṇo
yamhi saccañ ca dhammo ca so sucī so ca brāhmaṇo

388

Because a man has discarded all evil, he is called a Brāhman; because of his balanced conduct, he is called a monk (*samaṇa*); because he has rid himself of all impurities, he is called a recluse (*pabbajita*).

Note – The impurities are ten in number: greed, hate, delusion, conceit, speculative views, doubt, mental torpor, restlessness, shamelessness, and lack of moral scruples.

389

One should not strike a Brāhman; neither should a Brāhman give way to anger against him who strikes. Woe to him who slays a Brāhman; but greater woe to the Brāhman who vents his wrath (on the aggressor).

390

It is no small advantage to a Brāhman to restrain the mind from clinging to pleasurable things. In proportion to the degree that he abstains from wishing to injure others, to that degree will suffering cease.

391

He who has not committed unwholesome deeds through body, speech, or mind, and who is restrained in these three avenues – him I call a Brāhman.

392

Even as the (orthodox) Brāhman bows down to the sacrificial fire, so one should make obeisance to him who understands the Dhamma as proclaimed by the Fully Enlightened One.

393

Not by matted hair, by lineage, nor by birth (caste) does one become a Brāhman. But the one in whom there abide truth and righteousness, he is pure; he is a Brāhman.

394

kiṃ te jaṭāhi dummedha kin te ajinasāṭiyā?
abbhantaraṃ te gahanaṃ bāhiraṃ parimajjasi

395

paṃsukūladharaṃ jantuṃ kisaṃ dhamanisanthataṃ
ekaṃ vanasmiṃ jhāyantaṃ tam ahaṃ brūmi brāhmaṇaṃ

396

na câhaṃ brāhmaṇaṃ brūmi yonijaṃ mattisambhavaṃ
bhovādi nāma so hoti sace hoti sakiñcano
akiñcanaṃ anādānaṃ tam ahaṃ brūmi brāhmaṇaṃ

Note – Bhovādi is a familiar form of address used by the Brāhmans during the time of Buddha for equals and for inferiors. When the haughty Brāhmans and Jains came to discuss metaphysical problems

397

sabbasaṃyojanaṃ chetvā yo ce na paritassati
saṅgātigaṃ visaṃyuttaṃ tam ahaṃ brūmi brāhmaṇaṃ

398

chetvā nandiṃ varattañ ca sandāmaṃ sahanukkamaṃ
ukkhittapaḷighaṃ buddhaṃ tam ahaṃ brūmi brāhmaṇaṃ

394

O fool, what is the use of matted hair, and to what avail is raiment made of antelope skin?* Outwardly you cleanse yourself, but within you is a jungle of passions.

395

He who wears the cast-off garments (of a hermit), who is emaciated with the veins of his body standing out, who is solitary and contemplative in the forest – him I call a Brāhman.

396

I do not call him a Brāhman merely because he is born in the caste of the noble ones, or of a Brāhman mother. If he is a possessor (of passions), he becomes known by the appellation *bhovādi.* But one who is free from possessions (craving) and from worldly attachments – him I call a Brāhman.

with the Buddha, they often addressed him simply, "Bho, Gotama!" Therefore, the Buddhists used to designate the Brāhmans by this appellation which involves a certain amount of contempt. *Bhovādin* literally means one who uses the term "bho!"

397

He who has cut off all impediments and does not tremble with fears, who has passed beyond attachments and is free from shackles – him I call a Brāhman.

398

He is enlightened who has cut the strap (of ill will) and the thong (of craving), who has broken the chain (of heretical views) with its appurtenances (latent tendencies), and has removed the crossbar (of ignorance) – him I call a Brāhman.

*Worn by forest-dwelling mendicants of ancient India.

399

akkosaṃ vadhabandhañ ca aduṭṭho yo titikkhati
khantībalaṃ balānīkaṃ tam ahaṃ brūmi brāhmaṇaṃ

400

akkodhanaṃ vatavantaṃ sīlavantaṃ anussutaṃ
dantaṃ antimasarīraṃ tam ahaṃ brūmi brāhmaṇaṃ

401

vāri pokkharapatte'va āragger'iva sāsapo
yo na lippati kāmesu tam ahaṃ brūmi brāhmaṇaṃ

402

yo dukkhassa pajānāti idhe'va khayamattano
pannabhāraṃ visaṃyuttaṃ tam ahaṃ brūmi brāhmaṇaṃ

403

gambhīrapaññaṃ medhāviṃ maggāmaggassa kovidaṃ
uttamatthaṃ anuppattaṃ tam ahaṃ brūmi brāhmaṇaṃ

404

asaṃsaṭṭhaṃ gahaṭṭhehi anāgārehi c'ûbhayaṃ
anokasāriṃ appicchaṃ tam ahaṃ brūmi brāhmaṇaṃ

405

nidhāya daṇḍaṃ bhūtesu tasesu thāvaresu ca
yo na hanti na ghāteti tam ahaṃ brūmi brāhmaṇaṃ

399

He who with forgiveness bears up under reproach, abuse and punishment, and who looks upon patience as his army and strength as his force – him I call a Brāhman.

400

He who is free from anger, who vigilantly performs his religious practices, who is virtuous, pure, self-restrained, and bears his physical body for the last time – him I call a Brāhman.

401

He who, like water on a lotus leaf, or a mustard seed on the point of an awl, does not cling to sensuous pleasures – him I call a Brāhman.

402

He who while in this world realizes the end of his suffering, who has laid aside the burden (of his skandhas) and is free from attachments – him I call a Brāhman.

403

He whose wisdom is deep, who is expert in knowledge and in discerning the right from the wrong path; he who has realized the supreme goal – him I call a Brāhman.

404

He who does not associate closely either with householders (laymen) or with the homeless (mendicants), who does not frequent houses and who is content with few wants – him I call a Brāhman.

405

He who has laid aside the cudgel that injures any creature whether moving or still, who neither slays nor causes to be slain – him I call a Brāhman.

406

aviruddhaṃ viruddhesu attadaṇḍesu nibbutaṃ
sādānesu anādānaṃ tam ahaṃ brūmi brāhmaṇaṃ

407

yassa rāgo ca doso ca māno makkho ca pātito
sāsapor'iva āraggā tam ahaṃ brūmi brāhmaṇaṃ

408

akakkasaṃ viññāpaniṃ giraṃ saccaṃ udīraye
yāya nâbhisaje kiñci tam ahaṃ brūmi brāhmaṇaṃ

409

yo'dha dīghaṃ vā rassaṃ vā
aṇuṃ thūlaṃ subhâsubhaṃ
loke adinnaṃ nâdiyati
tam ahaṃ brūmi brāhmaṇaṃ

410

āsā yassa na vijjanti asmiṃ loke paramhi ca
nirāsayaṃ visaṃyuttaṃ tam ahaṃ brūmi brāhmaṇaṃ

411

yassâlayā na vijjanti aññāya akathaṅkathī
amatogadhaṃ anuppattaṃ tam ahaṃ brūmi brāhmaṇaṃ

412

yo'dha puññañ ca pāpañ ca ubho saṅgaṃ upaccagā
asokaṃ virajaṃ suddhaṃ tam ahaṃ brūmi brāhmaṇaṃ

406

He who is tolerant amongst the intolerant, who is calm amongst the violent, and who is unattached amongst those who are attached – him I call a Brāhman.

407

The one from whom lust and hatred, pride and hypocrisy have fallen away, like a mustard seed from the point of an awl – him I call a Brāhman.

408

He who speaks gentle, instructive and truthful words, whose utterances offend no one – him I call a Brāhman.

409

He who takes no object in this world that is not given to him, be it short or long, small or great, fair or ugly – him I call a Brāhman.

410

He who has no desires regarding this world or the next, who is free of longings and without fetters – him I call a Brāhman.

411

He who is free from craving and free from doubt through the realization of truth, and who has reached the depth of the deathless state (nirvana) – him I call a Brāhman.

412

He who has transcended the bonds of both merit and demerit, who is sorrowless, free from passions, and pure – him I call a Brāhman.

413

candaṃ'va vimalaṃ suddhaṃ vippasannamanāvilaṃ
nandībhavaparikkhīṇaṃ tam ahaṃ brūmi brāhmaṇaṃ

414

yo imaṃ paḷipathaṃ duggaṃ saṃsāraṃ mohamaccagā
tiṇṇo pāragato jhāyī anejo akathaṅkathī
anupādāya nibbuto tam ahaṃ brūmi brāhmaṇaṃ

415

yo'dha kāme pahatvāna anāgāro paribbaje
kāmabhavaparikkhīṇaṃ tam ahaṃ brūmi brāhmaṇaṃ

416

yo'dha taṇhaṃ pahatvāna anāgāro paribbaje
taṇhābhavaparikkhīṇaṃ tam ahaṃ brūmi brāhmaṇaṃ

417

hitvā mānusakaṃ yogaṃ dibbaṃ yogaṃ upaccagā
sabbayogavisaṃyuttaṃ tam ahaṃ brūmi brāhmaṇaṃ

418

hitvā ratiñ ca aratiñ ca sītibhūtaṃ nirūpadhiṃ
sabbalokābhibhuṃ vīraṃ tam ahaṃ brūmi brāhmaṇaṃ

413

He who like the moon, is stainless, pure, serene and unruffled, in whom desire for existence is extinguished – him I call a Brāhman.

414

He who has traversed this miry path of saṃsāra, difficult to pass; who has rid himself of delusion, crossed over and reached the other shore; who is absorbed in contemplation, free from craving and doubts, not grasping, and inwardly calm — him I call a Brāhman.

415

He who in this world has relinquished all sensuous pleasures, wanders homeless (for the welfare of the many), and has destroyed all desire (*kāma*) for existence — him I call a Brāhman.

416

He who in this world has extinguished all craving, wanders homeless, and has destroyed all thirst (*taṇhā*) for existence – him I call a Brāhman.

417

He who has abandoned all human ties and transcended even the celestial ties; who is truly free from all attachments – him I call a Brāhman.

418

He who has put aside what gives pleasure as well as what gives pain, who is passionless and free from the causal seeds of existence (*nirūpadhi*), the hero who has conquered all the worlds — him I call a Brāhman.

419

cutiṃ yo vedi sattānaṃ upapattiñ ca sabbaso
asattaṃ sugataṃ buddhaṃ tam ahaṃ brūmi brāhmaṇaṃ

420

yassa gatiṃ na jānanti devā gandhabbamānusā
khīṇāsavaṃ arahantaṃ tam ahaṃ brūmi brāhmaṇaṃ

421

yassa pure ca pacchā ca majjhe ca n'atthi kiñcanaṃ
akiñcanaṃ anādānaṃ tam ahaṃ brūmi brāhmaṇaṃ

422

usabhaṃ pavaraṃ vīraṃ mahesiṃ vijitāvinaṃ
anejaṃ nahātakaṃ buddhaṃ tam ahaṃ brūmi brāhmaṇaṃ

423

pubbenivāsaṃ yo vedī saggâpāyañ ca passati
atho jātikkhayaṃ patto abhiññāvosito muni
sabbavositavosānaṃ tam ahaṃ brūmi brāhmaṇan'ti

DHAMMAPADAṂ NIṬṬHITAṂ

419

He who has all knowledge concerning the death and rebirth of all beings, is unattached, who is content in himself (*sugata*), and enlightened (*buddha*) — him I call a Brāhman.

420

He whose path is unknown to devas, gandharvas and men, who has nullified all sensuous influxes and is a Holy One (*arahant*) — him I call a Brāhman.

421

He who has no longing for what is ahead, behind, or in the middle, who possesses nothing and is attached to nothing – him I call a Brāhman.

422

He who is fearless (as a bull), distinguished and heroic, a great sage, a conqueror; who is entirely free from craving and who has washed off all impurities, an Enlightened One — him I call a Brāhman.

423

He who knows his former abodes (his lives), who perceives (through spiritual insight) both heaven and hell, who has reached the end of all births, who has perfected himself in wisdom; such a sage who has accomplished all that ought to be accomplished (on the sublime path) – him I call a Brāhman.

THUS ENDS THE DHAMMAPADA

GLOSSARY

Commonly used Pāli terms and their Sanskrit equivalents.*

In the transliteration of both Pāli and Sanskrit, the character *c* represents the sound *ch* as in the English word chair. The aspirate consonants (kh, th, ph, etc.) are pronounced (as in blockhead or godhead).

Pāli	Sanskrit	Meaning	Verse
accuta	*acyuta*	permanent, imperishable (lit., unscattered, unfallen)	225
ādicca-(patha)	*āditya*	(path of) the sun	175
aggi	*agni*	fire	107, 136, 392
ahiṃsā	(same)	harmlessness, nonviolence	261, 270, 300
ākāsa	*ākāśa*	"shining": sky, space, ether	92, 175, 254
akkhara	*akshara*	science of sounds, phonetics; also imperishable	352
amata	*amṛita*	immortality	21
anattā	*anātman*	nonself	279

*Many words that are similar in Pāli and Sanskrit have in the course of time acquired divergent connotations. This Glossary is intended merely to aid readers, who have some acquaintance with Sanskrit philosophical terms, to recognize their etymological parallels in the Pāli text of the *Dhammapada*.

Pāli	Sanskrit	Meaning	Verse
appamāda	*apramāda*	vigilance, conscientiousness	Canto II
arahant	*arhant, arhat*	worthy; the worthy one	Canto VII
ariya	*ārya*	noble	22, 164, 208
atta(n)	*ātman*	self	Canto XII
avijjā	*avidyā*	ignorance	243
bāla	(same)	orig. young, unable to speak; ignorant, foolish*	Canto V
bhadra	(same)	auspicious, lucky, fortunate	119-20, 143
bhikkhu	*bhikshu*	mendicant, monk	Canto XXV
brahmacārin	(same)	leading a pure and holy life; a celibate student	142
brāhmaṇa	(same)	one who leads a pure, ascetic life	Canto XXVI
buddha	(same)	enlightened	passim
Buddha	(same)	Awakened One, Enlightened One	passim
cakka	*cakra*	wheel	1

*In Sanskrit *bāla* means a boy or young one. In Pāli, however, Buddha used the word to denote a childish person, by extension, a fool; for boy or child he used *bālaka*.

Pāli	Sanskrit	Meaning	Verse
canda	*candra*	the moon	172-3, 413
candimā	*candramas*	luminous, shiny; the moon	172, 208, 387
chāyā	(same)	shadow	2
citta	*citra*	to be bright, resplendent	151, 171
citta	(same)	heart, mind, attentiveness	Canto III
daḷha	*dṛḍha* (*dṛḷha*)	resolute, strong (to hold fast, bind)	23, 61, 112, 313
daṇḍa	(same)	rod, stick	Canto X
dassana	*darśana*	sight, vision	206, 210
adassana		blindness, not seeing	210
deva	(same)	god, divine being	105, 420
dhamma	*dharma*	"foundation, support": law, justice, doctrine, nature, truth, morality, and good conduct	passim
dhamma-ṭṭha	*dharma-stha*	standing in the *dhamma,* just, righteous	Canto XIX
dhuva	*dhruva*	permanent, constant (also name of the Pole Star)	147
dosa	*dośa*	anger, ill will; see *rāga* and *moha;* cf. *nibbāna*	20, 251
dukkha	*duḥkha*	pain, suffering, dis-ease, discord	passim

PĀLI	SANSKRIT	MEANING	VERSE
gandhabba	*gandharva*	heavenly musician: angelic being, demigod	105, 420
gutta	*gupta*	guarded, protected	passim
haṃsa	(same)	swan, goose	175
hiṃsā	(same)	injury, hurting, killing	132
iddhi	*ṛiddhi, siddhi*	potency, accomplishment; psychic power(s)	175
jana	(same)	creature, entity, people	99, 249, 320
jarā	(same)	old age, decrepitude	Canto XI
jhāna	*dhyāna*	meditation, thought, reflection	181, 372
kāma	(same)	desire	48, 186-7, 401, 415
kamma	*karman*	doing, action, result of action	passim
kāsāva, kāsāya	*kāshāya*	"brown": yellow robe of a Buddhist monk	9-10
khandha	*skandha*	collection, mass, aggregates: "elements of sensory existence"	374
khanti(ī)	*kshānti*	patience, forbearance, forgiveness	184, 399
khattiya	*kshatriya*	warrior or ruling caste	294
khetta	*kshetra*	field	356-9

Pāli	Sanskrit	Meaning	Verse
kodha	*krodha*	anger	Canto XVII
loka	(same)	space, world	44, 45, Canto XIII
macca	*martya*	mortal	53, 141, 182
maccu	*mṛityu*	death; also god of death; cf. *māra, yama*	passim
magga	*mārga*	path	Canto XX
mala	(same)	impurity, stain, dirt	239, 243
mana(s)	*manas*	mind	1, 2
māra	(same)	death, the evil one, tempter	passim
metta	*maitra (mitra)*	compassionate, friendly, benevolent	368
micchā-diṭṭhi	*mithyā-dṛishṭi*	wrong views, heresy	167, 316
moha	(same)	delusion, folly; see *dosa, rāga;* cf. *nibbāna*	20, 251
mokkha	*moksha*	release, freedom, emancipation; the final deliverance	37
mutta	*mukta*	freed, set free from worldly existence	20, 90, 348
nāga	(same)	serpent, elephant of great stature	Canto XXIII

PĀLI	SANSKRIT	MEANING	VERSE
nibbāna	*nirvāṇa*[*]	dousing (of a flame), dying out of *rāga, dosa,* and *moha,* the three basic character defects	passim
nicca	*nitya*	constant, perpetual	23, 109, 206, 293
niraya	(same)	destruction, hell	Canto XXII passim
pabbajita	*pravrājita*	a homeless monk	74, 388
pada	*pad, pād*	foot, step, path, track	179, 273
pakiṇṇaka	*pakīrṇaka*	scattered, miscellaneous	Canto XXI
pāna	*prāṇa*	breath of life, vitality	246-7
paṇḍita	(same)	wise, sage; pandit	Canto VI
paññā	*prajñā*	intelligence, wisdom, insight	38, 111, 152, 372
paññāsīla	*prajñāśīla*	higher intelligence and virtue	229
pāpa	(same)	suffering, evil	Canto IX
parinib-bāna	*parinirvāṇa*	complete extinction of *khanda*-life; final release of an Arhat after destruction of physical body	89

[*]This is not a negative state, but a condition beyond ordinary comprehension. It is the annihilation of craving, hatred, and ignorance.

Pāli	Sanskrit	Meaning	Verse
Pāṭi-mokkha	*Prati-moksha*	monastic precepts; discipline (Vinaya) for monks	185, 375
phala	(same)	ripe fruit, result, consequence	66, 178
piya	*priya*	dear, friend, amiable	Canto XVI
pūjā	(same)	honor, reverence, devotion	73, 106-7
puppha	*pushpa*	flower	Canto IV
putta	*putra*	son, young of animal, offspring	62, 84, 345
rāga	(same)	passion, lust; see *dosa* and *moha;* cf. *nibbāna*	20, 251
rājā	(same)	king	295
sabba	*sarva*	all, whole	129-30, 183, 353-4
sacca	*satya*	real, true; truth	393, 408
saddhā	*śraddhā*	faith, trust, devotion	8, 144
assaddha		not credulous or dependent on faith	97
sādhu	(same)	virtuous, honorable, meritorious	35, 67-8, 206
sagga	*svarga*	heaven	174
sahassa	*sahasra*	a thousand	Canto VIII

Pāli	Sanskrit	Meaning	Verse
samādhi	(same)	concentration; exalted state of consciousness	271
samaṇa	*śramaṇa*	religious recluse	184, 265
saṃsāra	(same)	"moving about continuously": the chain of births and deaths	95, 302, 414
saññojana *saṃyojana*	*saṃyojana*	fetters that bind one to the wheel of rebirth	221
sarīra	*śarīra*	physical body	151
sota	*srotas*	stream	339-40
Sugata	(same)	"happily gone": after death; faring well; Buddha	18, 419
sukha	(same)	happy, pleasant, blessed	118, 194, Canto XV, 331
sukka	*śukla*	light, pure, bright, white	87
suññatā	*śūnyatā*	emptiness, the Void *(nibbāna)*	92
taṇhā	*tṛishṇā*	thirst, craving	154, 334, 349
ṭhāna	*sthāna*	condition, state, stance	137, 225
vācā	*vāk, vāc*	voice, word, speech	232, 281
vagga	*varga*	chapter, section	all chapter headings
vaṇa	*vraṇa*	wound, sore	124

PĀLI	SANSKRIT	MEANING	VERSE
vana	(same)	forest, jungle (of desires)	283-4, 324, 344
vijāna	(same)	understanding, knowing	6, 64-5
viññāna	*vijñāna*	cognition, consciousness; one of the five *khandhas*	41
viriya	*vīrya*	vigor, energy, exertion	112
yama	(same)	god of death	passim
yamaka	(same)	double, twin	Canto I
yoga	(same)	"yoke": connection, bond, means	282, 417

THE FOUR NOBLE TRUTHS

PĀLI	SANSKRIT	MEANING
cattāri ariyasaccāni	*catvāri āryasatyāni*	four noble truths
1) *dukkha*	*duḥkha*	ill, pain, sorrow
2) *samudaya*	(same)	origin, cause of ill
3) *nirodha*	(same)	destruction of ill, cessation of ill
4) *magga*	*mārga*	road, way

THE NOBLE EIGHTFOLD PATH

PĀLI	SANSKRIT	MEANING
ariya aṭṭhaṅgika magga	*āryāshṭāṅga mārga*	noble eightfold path
1) *sammādiṭṭhi*	*samyagdṛishṭi*	right insight, right understanding, right vision
2) *sammāsaṃkappa*	*samyaksaṃkalpa*	right aspiration, right thoughts*
3) *sammāvācā*	*samyagvāc*	right speech
4) *sammākammanta*	*samyakkarmānta*	right action
5) *sammājīva*	*samyagājīva*	right livelihood, right living
6) *sammāvāyāma*	*samyagvyāyāma*	right effort
7) *sammāsati*	*samyaksmṛiti*	right memory, right mindfulness
8) *sammāsamādhi*	*samyaksamādhi*	right concentration

*Right thoughts in the Theravāda terminology denote the thoughts free from ill will, hatred, and jealousy.

APPENDIX

Dhammapada palm leaf manuscripts (750-1815 A.D.)

The following are some of the rarest *Dhammapada* manuscripts, their commentaries, subcommentaries, and also commentaries on commentaries, with the monastery libraries where they are housed. The translator elected to visit the easily accessible Vihāra libraries. The student may be interested to note that there are more than 950 recognized monastery libraries where he may find other compilations on *Dhammapada* which have never seen the light in print. Even in the British Library are different compilations of this scripture; and photostat copies of them may be obtained in Sinhalese script, Burmese script, or in Cambodian characters. Their reference numbers are:

a) Sinhalese-Pāli, I - 151 b and II - 551 W II (I).

b) Burmese, leaves 126 (K-T) Or 6454 A.P.

c) Cambodian characters, 360 leaves incomplete Or 1273 P.

I. *Dhammapadaṃ* (Pāli)

Subadrārāma Vihāra Monastery of Rt. Venerable Dharmapāla Nāyaka Thera, Batapola
Abhinavāramaya, Kosgoda
Pushparāma Mahā Vihāraya, Balapitiya

There are more than 236 monastery libraries where palm leaf manuscripts of this work are preserved.

II. *Dhampiyā* (Sinhalese)

Totagamu Raja Mahā Vihāraya, Telwatta
Rankoth Vihāraya, Ambalangoda
Gintota Purāna Pirivena, Gintota, near Galle

III. *Dhammapada Attha Kathā* (commentary on the legends of *Dhammapada*)

Gangārāma Vihāraya, Pitigala
Bodhimalu Raja Mahā Vihāraya, Bentota
Siri Sobhanārāmaya, Kahawa, Telwatta
This text is available also in 265 other monastery libraries.

IV. *Dhammapada Sannaya* (verbatim Sinhalese translation of *Dhammapada* with the Pāli text)

Paramānanda Vihāraya, Minuwangoda, Galle
Thūparāmaya, Gintota
Vijayānanda Mahā Vihāraya, Galle
The same palm leaf manuscript is available at 230 other monastery libraries.

V. *Dhammapada Vyākhyāva* (commentary on *Dhammapada*)

Svetabimbārāmaya, Bope, Galle
Ahangama Mahā Vihāraya, Ahangama
Saddharmākara Pirivena, Pinwatta, Panadura
Available at eight other monastery libraries.

VI. *Dhammapada Varnanā* (explanatory commentary on *Dhammapada* in Sinhalese)

Vevurukannala Mahā Vihāraya, Dikwella
Ambarikkārāmaya, Balapitiya
Nāradda Purāna Vihāraya, Hakmana
Available at about four other monastery libraries.

VII. *Dhammapada Kathā* (*Dhammapada* stories)
Ratna-Giri Purāna Vihāraya, Ganegama, Baddegama

Sudarshanārāma, Denipitiya
Jayamahā Vihāraya, Rekawa, Netolpitiya

There are only two other places where the palm leaf manuscript of this work is available.

VIII. *Dhammapada Atuvāva* (Sinhalese commentary on *Dhammapada*)

Abayasinhārāmaya, Maradana, Colombo
Sailabimbārāmaya, Dodanduwa
Ānandāramaya, Kitulampitiya, Galle

There are more than 270 other monasteries where palm leaf manuscripts of this work are housed.

IX. *Dhammapada Purāna Sannaya* (ancient Sinhalese commentary on *Dhammapada*)

Ganegodalle Raja Mahā Vihāraya, Kosgoda
Jetavana Pirivena Raja Mahā Vihāraya, Akuressa

There are only two places where this work is available.

X. *Dhammapada Gāthā Desu Aya* (individuals to whom the *Dhammapada* Gāthās were preached)

Only one copy of this palm leaf manuscript is available. It is housed in the monastery library of Nyagrodhārāmaya, Gonapeenuwala, Hikkaduwa.

XI. *Dhammapada Vistara Sannaya* (a comprehensive verbatim Sinhalese rendition with copious notes)

This rare manuscript is available only at the monastery library of Sunandārāma Vihāraya, Unawatuna, Galle.

by thinking carefully about their nature; however, Thomas Hobbes and John Rawls claim that we must first look at the sorts of relationships humans form and then determine the good accordingly. Finally, there are others, such as existentialists Albert Camus and Jean-Paul Sartre, who argue that there is no final good apart from life itself.

Although the disparities among these various philosophers are obvious, their intellectual journeys share a common element. Therefore, we begin our inquiries into the broad array of ethical questions by asking what we *should* be doing or working toward. That is, unlike sociology, ethics and morality are *prescriptive,* rather than *descriptive,* disciplines. In other words, they purport to say what people *ought* to do rather than merely describing how they do in fact behave. This is most explicit with regard to morality—a set of rules stating what you ought and ought not to do. But it is also true (in a less straightforward sense) in the field of ethical theory. For, in ethical inquiries, we should ask which values ought to be promoted, what sort of a person we should strive to be, and what kind of life we ought to pursue. As such, the study of ethics is more general than specific moral questions, but it nevertheless prescribes rather than simply describes.

A final point about the question of what the *summum bonum* is: It provides a starting point. If we can determine a best good, so to speak (and not all the authors included here believe that we can), this will provide a framework within which to begin to answer further questions. What is the ideal society? That which best enables its members to achieve the *summum bonum.* Who is the good person? He or she who comes closest to embodying, and facilitating others to realize, the greatest good. What rules (moral and legal) ought we to have? Those which promote the *summum bonum.*

ETHICS AND RELIGION

Ethics and religion, and philosophy and religion more generally, share a common heritage. Both philosophy and religion represent attempts to answer the biggest and the most basic human questions: How should one live one's life? What is the right thing to do? What is the meaning of life? Ethics, and the subject matter of this book, is particularly concerned with the first two questions, but it is virtually impossible to imagine answering them without first getting some grasp of the third, and some would say ultimate, question. The many and various religions of the world are the oldest attempts to provide some picture of the universe as a whole and, most important, to discern the meaning of it all. Many religions, of course, are allegorical, mythological, or metaphorical, but they all contain some core of concern for the significance of each individual life and the duties and obligations of each and every individual. What we call Judeo-Christian morality is the core of Judaism and Christianity respectively, and the core of Islam consists of a similar set of basic duties and obligations. The great religions of South and East Asia similarly present us with a set of duties and obligations derivative of their (sometimes very different) ways of looking at the universe. One of the most important differences between the religions, of course, is the centrality of beliefs about the existence and nature of God, or gods. There are religions without any such beliefs or in which such beliefs are of marginal importance (Buddhism and Confucianism, for example), and there are religions in which the belief in one (and only one) God is of central importance—notably in Judaism, Christianity, and Islam. But it is worth noting that even in the three great Western religions, there are sects and movements that try to hold onto the ethical core even while expressing doubts about the existence of God. For instance, there is a "death of God" movement that periodically arises in Christianity and some radical strands of "liberation theology" within the Catholic Church. This means that the various religions might be considered first in terms of ethics, their instructions to their members regarding the right way to live. In many cases what makes the right way to live right is its recommendation or approval by God or by gods, but it is important to allow for the possibility that there are other, independent reasons why what is right is right that may extend beyond the bounds of religious belief. But we have started this edition of our book with a consideration of the ethics of several of the world's great religions, not only Judaism, Christianity, and Islam, but Buddhism, Taoism, and Confucianism as well.

THE HISTORY OF ETHICS

It is of more than casual interest that some of the classical ethical statements that we will be studying in this book were written by philosophers who lived in cultures quite different (but not entirely different) from our own. Plato and Aristotle, most notably, wrote almost 2,500 years ago, in the city-state *(polis)* of Athens. On the one hand, their ethics are sufficiently similar to ours (and often taken as an ideal by modern thinkers) so that they are traditionally treated as the originators of ethical philosophy, and much of ethics since is based on them. Indeed, the whole history of ethics (and philosophy in general) has been said to be the development of ideas originally suggested by Plato and Aristotle so long ago, and much of what we will see in the texts of this book will be a continuing dialogue with these two great philosophers on a number of topics of mutual interest over the years. At the same time, however, the differences between our societies are sufficiently remarkable—the differences in whom they considered to be "the good man," for example—to make us think quite seriously about our own sense of the virtues.

Other writers are more modern but still quite distinctly different from ourselves and from each other. Both Immanuel Kant and Friedrich Nietzsche, for example, are German writers from the previous two centuries (Kant died as an old man in 1804; Nietzsche died relatively young in 1900), but even the 100-year difference that separates them is more than sufficient to display drastic differences in outlook. Kant insists that there is a universal set of absolute moral rules, whereas Nietzsche, heralding in the twentieth century, warns us of a breakdown in traditional moral codes and anticipates the individualistic ethical codes that have become so prevalent today. Indeed, even French author, "existentialist" Jean-Paul Sartre, writing only 40 years ago, gives us a quite different picture of the world than most of us would recognize today. But his was the world of Paris under the Nazi occupation, in which the outlook was bleak but nevertheless heroic, in which individual acts of resistance could mean a great deal, and in which even the smallest gesture of defiance counted as a sign of hope. Finally, John Rawls addresses some of the problems facing contemporary (capitalist) society.

What Is the Good Life?

The Danish philosopher Søren Kierkegaard wrote in his *Journals,* when he was a young man of 20 or so, "I want a truth for which I can live and die." He was asking the ultimate ethical question, What is worth living for? Indeed this has been the motivating question for almost every great (and not so great) philosopher, the question of the meaning of life, the problem of choosing between a variety of alternatives—some of which (but we don't know which) will make our lives fulfilled and admirable, and others will make us miserable and, perhaps, damned as well. The most dramatic presentation of this question in the history of philosophy is the dilemma of Socrates, in 399 B.C. He was already an old man of 70, and he had made a considerable reputation (and nuisance of himself) challenging the assumptions of the politicians and judges of Athens. In doing so, he made many enemies, and, finally, he was accused of "corrupting the minds" of the young students he was teaching and was sentenced to death. In prison, Socrates had a chance to escape. He also knew that he had done right and had been treated unfairly by the court. (In his own speech to the judges, he had humorously suggested that as punishment, the state should provide him with free meals in the public square, a privilege normally reserved for victorious Olympic athletes.) He thus faced an ultimate choice—to turn down the offer to escape and face his punishment as a good (if unfairly treated) citizen, or leave Athens for sanctuary elsewhere and continue to lead his own life with its pleasures and satisfactions. He chose to stay and be executed on the grounds that honor and citizenship are more important than even life itself. That which is most worth living for may also be worth dying for. (You will find Socrates's deliberations in Plato's *Crito,* pages 69 to 79.)

Somewhat more modest than the overriding question about what is worth living (or dying) for, the personal motivation behind much of ethics has been the search for the good life, a life well lived. The problem, as Aristotle pointed out in his *Ethics* (pages 108 to 146), is that there are many different conceptions of the good life, and it is not at all clear which, if any, is the best. For example, there is the life of pleasure (also called *hedonism*), which has often been a primary candidate for the good life. But there are different kinds of pleasures and, perhaps, different "qualities" of pleasure as well (as John Stuart Mill argues in his *Utilitarianism,* pages 318 to 369). The gluttonous pleasure of stuffing oneself with fast-food hamburgers is one thing; the more ethereal pleasures of reading poetry or listening to Mozart are of quite a different nature. But then there are a great many goals in our lives that may not be aimed at pleasure at all. For example, we have ambitions and want to be successful, and though we may want success in order to give us pleasure, it is more likely for a great many people that the work required for success at least postpones, if it does not interfere with, the life of pleasure. We feel obligations and do favors for other people, often without pleasure as our reward, and we abstain from behavior that we know would give us great pleasure, just because we know that it is wrong. Moreover, there are conceptions of life that are antithetical to the life of pleasure; for instance, there is a conception of the good life as the religious life, in which the "pleasures of the body" are to be foregone in favor of the "purity of spirit." Questions about the good life are thus attempts to order this variety of concerns according to some sort of priorities: Which is more important, a pleasant life or a successful one? Which is more important, to do what one thinks is right or to do what will advance one's own interests? To live an enjoyable life here on earth or to earn a place in Heaven? To be a respected part of the community and established in a career or to be "free"? To do work that one thinks is important or poetic or to earn as much money as possible? The good life is the life well lived, and every philosopher in this book has his own opinions about what that should be.

Why Be Good?—The Problem of Justification

The question, Why be moral? is a way of summing up the central quest for *justification* in ethics. To justify an action or a principle is to show that there is good reason for it—in fact, better reasons, perhaps, than there are for any alternatives. To justify quitting college, for example, an (ex-) student might cite such reasons as "being bored" or "wanting to see the world" or "wanting to spend more time with the working class in order to start the Revolution." Such reasons are attempted justifications, and whether they succeed depends on whether they are also good reasons and whether there are better reasons for the opposite action (in this case, staying in school).

Every attempt to order the various ingredients in the good life requires some sort of justification, some good reasons. For example, we might argue that all our actions are aimed at pleasure anyway (is this true?), so you might as well take pleasure explicitly as your goal in life and not bother with the rest. (Would this be a good reason?) You might try to justify being moral by arguing that doing good makes the world a better place to live in and ultimately benefits everyone, including yourself. (Is this true?—and if so, is there a problem in justifying morality with such reasons?) Many of our actions and rules are justifiable by straightforward prudential reasons; the rule that you shouldn't drive through red traffic lights is, first of all, based on the very good reason that a person who does so is likely to get killed. Many of our actions and rules are justifiable by straightforward social or aesthetic reasons; for example, we don't eat chili with our fingers because such behavior strikes most people with whom we are likely to eat as socially unacceptable and revolting. Very often a social reason consists of little more than "we just don't do it that way here (and if you don't like it, get out)." An aesthetic reason might stop with the insult, "Well, then, you just have bad taste."

It is in the arena of morality and moral reasons that the problem of justification becomes acute. Morality is by its very definition not so simply justified by an appeal to our own interests or well-being (which is not to say that we can't be happy and be moral). Moral reasons are something more than social reasons, first because we can override a social reason by showing that it is immoral. (We were not convinced, when apologists defended apartheid in South Africa, on the grounds that racial separation had "worked" in the past.) Second, we expect something more by way of an anchor for moral justification than a sociological observation. It is for this reason that morality and moral reasons are often anchored in the word of God or some other claim about the ultimate good.

Similarly, moral reasons are much stronger than aesthetic reasons; the prohibitions against murder and treason are not based on the fact that most people find such acts distasteful or even revolting. To say that an act is immoral is to condemn it in the strongest possible terms. We expect that the reasons behind such a condemnation will be equally strong.

What justifies a course of action? Sometimes, appeal to our own tastes or interests is sufficient (for example, when deciding to take an elective course or ordering lunch). When the interests of other people are affected (especially when such effects are negative), justification of our actions becomes far more complicated. It requires some sort of demonstration that the act is acceptable in spite of its detrimental effect on others. For instance, we might argue that it is our duty to perform the action in question, regardless of its effects on others. Or we could claim that although certain harms are involved, overall the action produces more good than harm. There are numerous other ways in which we might seek to justify an action, several of which we shall discuss in the final part of this introduction, and many of which we shall see through the classical sources included in this volume.

For now it is enough to point out the connection between the demand for justification and the ethical theories with which we shall be concerned. To demand justification is first and foremost to ask *why.* We might ask why a person is entitled to or warranted in acting that way. Or we might put it in terms of questioning why we ought not to blame the person for so acting. (The two basically come to the same thing.) In either case, what we are demanding is an answer that goes beyond the individual's own tastes, desires, or goals. In so doing, what we are looking for is a *principle* that supports or justifies the act regardless of the personal interests of the person performing it. Roughly speaking, the choice of principles that you accept as the basis for justification will form the basis of your ethical theory.

Why Be Rational?—The Place of Reason in Ethics

Our discussion of justification and reasons in ethics underscores our insistence that we are not only concerned with doing right but with doing right because it is right and for the right reasons. It is not enough to be a moral hero who foils the bank robbery inadvertently (by driving through a red light and causing an accident, for example). To do good and to be moral require doing so for reasons and for the right kind of reasons. ("Because I just felt like it" would usually not be such a reason; "because I believed that it was the right thing to do," while incomplete, would at least be the beginning of the right kind of reason.) Thus some philosophers—Aristotle and Kant, for example—take ethics to be an essentially *rational* enterprise. An act or a principle is justified by virtue of its reasons.

It is the importance of reasons in ethics that establishes the importance of theories in ethics as well. A moral theory is essentially an attempt to organize and ground the various sorts of reasons that justify our actions, from very particular reasons ("I did it because he had a gun") to the most general reasons ("everyone has a right to protect his or her own life"). For philosophers who insist that ethics is essentially rational, the presence of such reasons is essential to right action. Kant, for example, insists that an action has "moral worth" only if a person actually has the right reason for performing it in mind, as "respect for the law" or "because it is my duty."

There are other philosophers, however, who have challenged this primary place of reason in ethics. Some have said that reason has its limits; others have even said that reason has very little place in ethics. David Hume, for example, argued that ethics was not primarily a matter of rationality but rather of *sentiment,* emotion rather than reason. We can justify morality in a limited way, Hume argued, by showing how it "pleases" us, but in the strong sense of rationality required by many philosophers, morality is unjustifiable and irrational. ("'Tis not contrary to reason," Hume wrote in one of the works included here, "for me to prefer the destruction of the whole world to the scratching of my finger.") Nietzsche goes even further and argues that there has been too much emphasis on rationality in ethics and that reason, rather than being the key to the good life, is rather a symptom of failure in life, a desperate attempt to justify a life that fails to be full and satisfactory in its own terms. Sartre, in a very different way, argues that reason is mere wishful thinking and that the hard questions of ethical choice cannot be so easily and impersonally resolved.

Which Is Right?—Ethical Dilemmas

Much of the motivation for studying ethics comes from the need to resolve conflicts and put some order in your life, from the need to order the various ingredients in the good life to the conflict of reason and the passions just mentioned. But what makes ethics so difficult, and sometimes so unsatisfying, is the fact that not all conflicts seem easily resolvable, and perhaps some are not resolvable at all. For example, there is a recurrent antagonism between personal and prudential interests on the one hand, and moral, impersonal principles on the other. Is there a general way of ordering these, giving one absolute priority over the other? Furthermore, our own interests are often in conflict, and we can have conflicting obligations too, so that, whatever we do, we do something wrong. (Imagine that two friends desperately need your help, but that you are unable to help them both.) But, most complicated of all, sometimes whole moral systems contradict one another. One society absolutely forbids sex before marriage and another encourages it. One society treats abortion as murder and another allows abortions in the name of the general welfare. One society even condones murder as an expression of individual strength and power; another condemns any show of power and treats murder as the most heinous crime.

But although a single ethical system might provide some guideline for ordering principles and priorities, a clash of ethical systems forecloses any such possibility. Thus, some of the crucial questions of our time have to do not so much with the justification of one value system rather than another, but with the *coexistence* of several value systems (the phenomenon we call *pluralism*). How is this possible? How can one choose among them? Are all of them equally correct relative to a particular society? Here we face the problem of relativism (to which we shall return)—the thesis that values are correct only relative to a given culture (or subculture). It is one thing to point out (as an anthropologist might do) that a pluralist society has several sets of values and opinions about what is right; it is quite different to live in that society and have to choose between these different values and opinions. This again is a primary function of ethical theories—to provide us with a way of evaluating conflicting ethical viewpoints, not only with regard to particular cases but where competing ethical systems present us with very different pictures of morality and the good life.

Ethical dilemmas are particularly perplexing problems in ethics, sometimes involving whole systems of values as well as particular conflicts of values. The practice of abortion raises such a dilemma because it immediately brings into question some of the most general concerns and concepts of our value system, for example, the concern for individual right to life and the concept of what it is to be a human being. But the study of ethics is not restricted to these often dramatic dilemmas and conflicts; it is also concerned with the understanding and appreciation of the coherence and justification of our values. Ethical dilemmas bring these values into sharp focus, but the study of ethics itself is at least as concerned with what is right and essential about our ethics as it is with its difficulties and dilemmas.

ETHICAL CONCEPTS

Universality

We have seen that in attempting to morally justify action, it is often held to be necessary to go beyond one's own interests and take into account the interests of others as well. There is, in other words, an aspect of fairness or impartiality that is generally taken to be a necessary feature of any moral system. To think impartially, in this sense, is to put yourself on an equal standing with others. It is, in other words, a refusal to allow your own interests privileged status. The universality requirement in ethics, then, is the application of the justifying principles to everyone (in the universe, so to speak) equally. Almost all the theories we will study do hold some sort of fairness, as guaranteed by principles that are universally applicable, to be essential.

Prudence and Morals

Prudence, in a phrase, is looking out for your own personal interests. It may be prudent "not to get involved"; it may be prudent to go to law school. In itself, prudence need not be *selfishness* (more on that later), but it does mean looking after your own interests whether or not they happen to be anyone else's interests too. It may be, as Aristotle and Mill and other philosophers suggest, that one's own interests also coincide with the interests of society. But prudence refers only to one's personal interests; other people's interests are a separate question.

Morality, on the other hand, always looks beyond our own interest to what is *right* or *required.* Morality will usually be concerned with other people's interests (as well as our own), but this is not necessarily so. Morality might refer to God's interests, for example, or to a well-established moral principle that might not seem to serve anyone's interests. Morality, unlike prudence, is necessarily *impersonal* in this sense and *objective.* That is, morality is not determined by the *subjective* (personal) attitudes of individuals but by some authority (whether it be God's will or society or reason itself). Moral authority does not belong to any particular person, no matter how powerful. (It may, however, belong to a particular person in a certain office, for example, as Pope or President or Imam.) It is concerned with rules, principles, and duties that have no reference to the desires, aspirations, interests, or power of any particular person, although particular people (for example, judges) may be guardians of morality. The moral principle "do not lie" applies to everyone, and it will not do to say, "but in my case, it's so much fun to lie" or "but when I lie to him he treats me so much better." Morality consists of impersonal demands that make no particular reference to individuals. ("John shouldn't lie" is not a moral principle; it is the application of a moral principle to John.) For this reason, contrary to a popular way of speaking, there is no such thing as a "personal morality."

Happiness and the Good

Prudence is looking out after your own interests—whatever those interests happen to be. *Happiness,* however, seems at one and the same time to be both a more specific concept—happiness seems to be a single feature of life—and a more general one—happiness also seems to be the satisfaction of all (or at least a great many) of our desires in life. Happiness, of course, need not be limited to the satisfaction of our own desires at all; our happiness may be completely bound up in the well-being of our family, or the success of our business firm, or the thriving of our community. Indeed, it might seem as if almost anything might make some people happy, which has led some authors to suggest that happiness is strictly subjective and depends only on the personal desires of the individual. On the other hand, some authors (Aristotle especially) have insisted that happiness is not merely subjective and a person can't be called "happy" unless he or she is also a good person, no matter how contented he or she might feel about life.

Whatever the scope of happiness, however, most authors seem to agree that it is one of the most important—if not the most important—thing in life. Aristotle tells us that "happiness" is the name of the ultimate goal—the *summum bonum*—of all of human life; it is the complete life, which could be no better. John Stuart Mill agrees (although he often conflates happiness and pleasure); it is happiness alone that moves people to act and happiness alone that can be the basis of morality and the good life. And John Rawls argues in our final selection that the just life is congruent with what people consider a happy life. This view of the harmonious relationship between morality and happiness is broken by Kant, who insists that happiness is one thing, morality something quite different. Kant agrees that what we all *want* in life is happiness, but he also insists that what we *ought* to do need not be what makes us happy.

What is happiness? Aristotle defines it as the Good itself, that is, "the good for man." But here we see the Good once again break into two parts, which weave in and out together throughout the history of ethics. There is the Good as in "the good life," whose aim is happiness, and there is the Good as in "a good person," whose concern is rather propriety and morality. When students are asked to draw up two lists, one in which they list the goals they would like to achieve in order to make them happy, the other a list of characteristics that they would find morally admirable, the lists are usually quite different, and one of the most troublesome questions in ethics is, Are they even compatible? In what ways are our goals and desires determined and delimited by our morals? And to what extent are our morals aimed at making us happy?

Egoism and Altruism

The contrast between prudence and morality is related to—but not identical to—the opposed concepts of *egoism* and *altruism.* Egoism, like prudence, means looking out for your own interests (although the word "egoism," unlike "prudence," suggests some essential antagonism between one's own interests and the interests of others). Altruism, however, means acting for the interests of others. Although morality need not be concerned with the interests of others (although it usually is), it is by its very nature impersonal; that is, it makes reference to no particular interests. Altruism, on the other hand, is precisely this concern for the interests of other people. It may be based on some sense of attachment or compassion, but it need not be. One could be altruistic on principle, though this might still not be the same as morality. Consider, for example, a person who was routinely altruistic just because he thought himself to be worthless and other people's interests more important. (Thus, several authors—including Aristotle, Kant, Rawls, and even Mill and Nietzsche—have argued that self-respect is an essential ingredient in any ethics.)

On the one hand, egoism is obviously antithetical to morality; it designates concern for our own interests, whatever the rules and whatever our obligations. (We can, of course, be moral and fulfill our obligations just as a means to satisfying our interests, but this is a complication we can postpone until later.) On the other hand, egoism has been argued by many ethicists to be the sole basis for any human behavior, moral or otherwise. This raises a very difficult question: If this is true, how is it possible to act for the sake of others (unless their interests coincide with our own) or for the sake of morality (unless our obligations also satisfy our interests)? Are we moral only because it is in our interests? If I give money to a beggar and feel good that I have done so, have I in fact given him the money only in order to feel good afterward? If I act virtuously out of self-respect (because I consider myself to be a kind person, for instance), am I thereby acting selfishly?

Philosophers sometimes distinguish between *psychological* egoism and *ethical* egoism. Psychological egoism is the psychological theory that everything we do, we do for our own interests, whether the same act serves other people's interests or moral obligations or not. Ethical egoism is the view that we *ought* to act in our own interests. Of course, if psychological egoism is true, then we could not help but act in our own interests. Nevertheless, the two positions are distinct. We might believe that all people are motivated by their own interests (psychological egoism) and nevertheless try to make sure that people's interests coincided with the common good and morality (for example, by inflicting punishments to offset any personal advantage in wrongdoing). And we might well believe that people are not naturally out for their own interests but that they ought to be (ethical egoism). Imagine a person who believes, for instance, that most of the damage done in the world is caused by "do-gooders" who "ought to leave well enough alone."

Altruism might also be divided into two parts, psychological altruism—the theory that people naturally act for the benefit of others—and ethical altruism—the view that they ought to act for the benefit of others. Regarding the first, many theorists have debated whether any of our actions are altruistically motivated, but very few have ever asserted that all of them are. The debate, therefore, centers around psychological egoism and the question whether all of our actions are self-interested. Ethical altruism, quite naturally, runs into questions about morality, and although the two concepts are different, the questions raised about their justification, for example, are essentially the same. The questions, Why should I be moral? and Why should I care about anyone else? are generally tackled together, and, for many practical purposes, they receive much the same set of answers.

According to a popular story, Abraham Lincoln was passing a puddle in a carriage when he saw that several little piglets were drowning as the mother pig squealed helplessly. Lincoln stopped the carriage and saved the piglets. (Whether the mother pig thanked him was not recorded.) Back on the road, Lincoln's friend asked him whether that act counted as a pure case of altruism. Lincoln replied, "Why that was the very essence of selfishness. I should have had no peace of mind all day."

Virtue and the Virtues

Morality is often defined as a set of principles (of a certain sort), but ethics is not just concerned with principles. In particular, ethics is also concerned with *character* and with personal charms and achievements, whether or not these fall under moral principles. The name traditionally given to such a positive feature of a person is a *virtue.* (A negative feature, in these terms, is a *vice.*) But, unfortunately, the confused history of morals has resulted in a confusing ambiguity for this crucial term. On the one hand, there is a particular feature of a person's character—such as honesty, wittiness, generosity, or social charm. On the other hand, there is that general all-encompassing designation of a person's virtue and talk of "virtue" in general as a synonym for "morality." (Kant, for example, uses the word "virtue" in this way.)

An ethics that focuses on the virtues has a very different emphasis than an ethics concerned with virtue (that is, morality). The first has mainly to do with character, with realizing one's potential and cultivating those habits that are essential to living in society. The second has more to do with following certain principles and less to do with character. A person might be virtuous in the second sense, for example, by dutifully resisting temptation and painfully managing not to do anything immoral. But, in the first sense, that person would not be exemplifying the virtues at all, for a virtue is not an inner wrestling match with one's desires; it is a cultivated habit that feels entirely natural. Whether it also obeys some principle is not at all a part of the description of the virtue.

Aristotle, we shall see, develops an ethics based on the virtues. He insists, first of all, that a person be raised correctly so that the virtues become regular habits. Only later, in the study of ethics, does a person learn to articulate the implicit principles in virtue of which such habits are good. A virtue, then, is a cultivated state of character. Virtue—in the Kantian sense of obeying moral principles—is more a matter of will than of habit and only secondarily, therefore, a question of character. (Good character, in this second sense, is as much a matter of will power as good habits.)

Facts and Values

A recurring problem in ethics is the apparent gap between value judgments and facts. It is true that we often justify moral claims by citing facts: "I claim that he has done wrong because he took money that didn't belong to him," or "I was right to take the money because he promised it to me." But there is always something less than entailment in such claims; we can add up the facts indefinitely, but no value conclusion seems to follow.

David Hume, remarking on this logical problem, summed it up as "the impossibility of deriving an 'ought' from an 'is'." In this century, the same phenomenon has been characterized by Cambridge philosopher G. E. Moore in his "Open Question Argument": namely, no matter how many facts about a thing you add together, the question is always open, Yes, but is it a *good* thing? Lists of facts do not yield values, and value judgments, in turn, can never be completely supported by the facts. But this has led to an awkward conclusion: Morality, and value judgments in general, cannot be ultimately justified. They can be derived from other value judgments, of course, but there is no factual anchor that can be used to justify them all. Thus, it can be argued that an ethical viewpoint—a vision of what the world ought to be—can be defended no matter what the facts. If a social reformer insists that people should be made into creatures quite different from what they are, appeals to the facts of human needs and desires and actual behavior will not change his or her mind.

This conclusion has not always been accepted or even seriously entertained in philosophy, no matter how frequently it is now argued. The Greek philosophers, for example, would have considered their ethical claims themselves to be factually true, and Augustine, to take a very different example, would say that a moral judgment is justified by the fact that it is based on the will of God. Even Kant—a vigorous defender of morality—accepts this harsh separation between facts and values, knowledge and morality. It is this apparent gap, accordingly, that makes the justification of morality so difficult. If solid facts won't do it, what will?

Justice and Equality

Of all the virtues, perhaps the most prominent—certainly in the good society but also in the moral individual—is *justice.* Socrates, Plato, Aristotle, and Rawls for example, praise it more than any other virtue and devote an extraordinary amount of attention to it. Justice is sometimes considered primarily a feature of social-political philosophy—an essential concern of governments and social critics. But it is also essential to ethics, to our sense of fair play and correct behavior in personal transactions.

Justice, first of all, is that sense of wrong that is invoked when someone (including ourselves) is cheated or unfairly taken advantage of. It is that sense that people who do wrong (even ourselves) should be punished and that those who do good (especially ourselves) should be rewarded. It is the belief that wealth or power should not give a person certain kinds of advantages, for example, "before the law"; and it is sometimes the belief that, although hard work and accomplishment are to be encouraged, those who are afflicted by misfortune and are unable to work ought to be reasonably taken care of by someone else. Justice, ultimately, is that quality of an act or of a whole society that conforms to our highest ideals of morality and fairness.

Central to this sense of justice is the concept of equality. This is not to say that one cannot have a sense of justice without believing in equality; both Plato and Aristotle believed in a most unequal society, in which slavery was a primary economic structure. But even they insisted on equality in a sense (similar cases should be treated similarly). Today, justice includes a presupposition of equality that might be stated, "Each person counts for one and for no more than one." This is not to say that everyone is the same. It is not to say, which is obviously false, that everyone has the same opportunities or abilities, and it is not to say that everyone should be treated the same, regardless of physical condition, age, abilities, ambitions, and interests. The sense of equality that is crucial here is a formal one; it means that everyone counts, and it means that, in respect to being a person, everyone should be treated the same. Thus, two people accused of the same crime should expect the same considerations in court, and two people to whom we owe money should expect the same prompt payment, even if one person is a dear friend and the other a not very likable acquaintance. The formal principle of equality is that everyone is the same in certain central respects, no matter who they are or what their station in life.

Many moral virtues and many of the demands of morality refer primarily to the activities or character of the individual; justice, on the other hand, has more to do with the interchange of life, giving and taking (including punishments), sharing and keeping for one's own. Justice is giving everyone his or her due, and the personal sense of justice is first of all making sure that we do not take more than our share, as well as making sure that we are not given less.

Rights and Duties

Although only three of our authors (Thomas Hobbes, John Stuart Mill, and John Rawls) explicitly make use of the concept of rights, many of the moral claims we might make can be refined by translating them into talk about rights and duties. For instance, in our discussion of justification, we saw that one way to defend our action is to claim to have been *entitled* to act so. And this is just another way of saying "I had a right to do that." But what is a right, and how do we know which ones we have? *Legal* rights—for instance, those listed in the Bill of Rights—are easy to identify (although not necessarily easy to interpret and apply) because they are explicitly stated in the Constitution. But legal rights are not the sort with which we are primarily concerned in ethics. Rather, the kind of rights to which we shall be appealing are *moral* rights, and they require much more by way of explanation or justification than simply pointing to a document.

Establishing the grounds for moral rights is a complicated business, however, and this is not the place for an extended discussion. It is enough to point again to the importance of justification and its connection with rights. For instance, both Kant and Rawls make use of the sense of equality in which all human beings are inherently equal and worthy. Rawls translates this intuition into the language of rights: "Each person is to have an equal right to the most extensive basic liberty compatible with a similar liberty for others." When we assert a right to be treated in a particular way (or to be left alone with regard to particular activities), we have to articulate and justify that area of our lives that is being protected. Thus, both Hobbes and Rawls begin with the intuitively appealing assertion of equality (although for very different reasons) and then proceed to derive a list of specific rights that we have as a result of this equality.

What is a right, and how does it work? Ronald Dworkin, a contemporary philosopher, has famously called rights "trumps." The idea is that, just as in a card game in which one suit is trump and wins over other suits, rights have a similar "last-word" function. For instance, although we might give a number of reasons for protesting a university policy, all we may really need to do to justify the action is to assert the right to free speech because, except in cases of imminent danger or other prohibited disruptions, that right protects our freedom to protest. Rights, then, offer protection. They establish a zone of freedom that is sacrosanct regardless of majority opinion, our past behavior, social status, or the circumstances (again, except for cases of imminent danger).

Duties, on the other hand, impose obligations. They are, however, intimately tied to rights. In order to have our rights respected, there must be limits (duties) on what others can do. For instance, my right to free speech is worthless unless you have (and everyone else has) a correlative duty to refrain from silencing me. Thus, duties are said to be the other side of rights; they are correlated to them. Although they are not always directly referred to as duties, many of the moral prohibitions and prescriptions we will talk about in this text can be translated into claims about the obligation to do or to refrain from doing something.

ETHICAL THEORIES AND APPROACHES

Finally, we review some of the major approaches used in the attempt to answer some of the problems we have discussed, as well as organizing and accounting for the values, duties, rights, and goals we might be taken to have. Not all of these are represented in the readings offered, because choices must inevitably be made given the vast amount of writings in the history of ethics, and also because this text is intended as an introduction through *classical sources.* Although such sources do not compose the whole of ethical theory, they are an essential first step in any attempt to come to grips with the discipline. The problems, discussions, and dialogues begun and continued by the authors in this book provide the material for those philosophers who have come after them, including those who radically disagree.

Teleology

One way to get around the gap between facts and values is to appeal morality to a peculiar kind of fact—the fact that something has a certain purpose. Thus, one can say that the value of the heart in an animal is the fact that its purpose is to pump the blood around the body. This raises a further question: What is the purpose of pumping the blood around the body? This too can be answered in terms of a purpose (to carry food and oxygen to the body, eliminate waste, etc.). Eventually, we reach an answer of the sort, to keep the creature alive, at which point we want to know, Is there some purpose to this? A practical if not very sentimental answer might be, Yes, we need it for food in the fall, or Yes, it has kittens who need her care. A more philosophical answer might be, Because every living thing has its place in nature. But when the creature in question is one of us, we have a very special interest in establishing some purpose for existence, and we have developed a series of powerful answers in terms of purposes—not particular purposes (such as "because I want to finish the semester") but ultimate purposes of the sort, "because this is the way the world is supposed to be."

The philosophical term for such purposive explanations and justifications is *teleology.* The word comes from the Greek word for purpose, *telos,* and a teleological justification of morality was attempted, most famously, by Aristotle, in the work included in this book. A teleological justification appeals the basic principles of morality, or an account of the virtues, to some overriding goal, built in to human nature or nature in general. We have already commented that Aristotle took this ultimate goal to be happiness, but we have not said that this goal is part of a much larger scheme of things in which Aristotle speculates upon the purpose of human existence and, ultimately, the purpose of the existence of the world. A teleological justification of morality, in other words, is a demonstration that our moral principles and behavior fit into some larger purpose. It might be an intrinsically human purpose. Or it might be a divine purpose, an expression of God's will. In Saint Augustine's work, for example, there is the classic statement of the view that the justification of morality depends on God. Accepting the same view, the Russian novelist Fyodor Dostoevsky has one of his characters (Ivan Karamazov) declare, "If there is no God, everything is permitted." It is a viewpoint that we shall see expressed, with a cheerful if perverse enthusiasm, by Friedrich Nietzsche and, with a kind of caution, by Jean-Paul Sartre. On the other hand, if there is a God, many people feel that this would provide an ultimate purpose—and a justification—for morality.

Utilitarianism

The most influential theory of justification of morality, in the past several centuries, has been the theory called *utilitarianism.* It is at once an ethical theory concerning the justification of morality and at the same time a formulation of the *summum bonum*—a single principle that will tell us how we ought to act. The basic formulation of utilitarianism is simply, "the greatest good for the greatest number," or what John Stuart Mill calls "the utility principle." It is a theory that is both impersonal and objective (insofar as we consider everyone's happiness and not just our own) and answers to our personal interests (because we are included in the "everyone"). Utilitarianism begins with the view that what motivates us can be only our own happiness, but it then derives the general principle (incorporating the universality requirement) that we ought therefore to act not just for our own happiness but for "the greatest good for the greatest number."

Utilitarianism, in one sense, goes back to the beginning of ethics (thus prompting Mill to proclaim that it has been presupposed by every moral philosopher). It is based on the generally acceptable view that morality requires that the interests of everyone should be taken into account and everyone wants to be happy. But utilitarianism as a particular ethical theory is much more specific than this; it is based on a very particular notion of "utility" (a concept that the Greeks, and later Nietzsche, considered "vulgar") and one modern notion of justice and equality. The notion of utility—although it often masquerades under the name "happiness"—is ultimately concerned with pleasure and pain, in discrete quantities that can be measured and compared. This modern notion of justice is the view that "each person counts for one and no more than one"; in other words, everyone's pleasure (and pain) is to count equally, and it is the overall amount of pleasure that determines what we ought to do. Morality is the general maximization of pleasure and the minimization of pain.

Utilitarianism had its origins in the "enlightenment" thinking of many eighteenth-century philosophers, including David Hume, who argues for the importance of utility in his *Inquiry Concerning the Principles of Morals* (included here). The founder of the utilitarian movement proper was an English reformer named Jeremy Bentham, who developed a "happiness calculus" to evaluate every action. For every course of action, we would add up all the various pleasures of everyone concerned, subtracting the amount of pain. We would compare that total with the amount resulting from alternative courses of action and then choose the course of action that maximized pleasure and minimized pain. Bentham's immediate aim was to reform the hopelessly complex and often cruel English legal system by developing a schedule of punishments that would just outweigh the pleasure of the wrongful act—thus minimizing the amount of pain to the smallest amount necessary to deter crime. But the theory also had general application as an overall ethical theory.

The ultimate champion of ethical utilitarianism was not Bentham but the son of James Mill, one of his colleagues. John Stuart Mill was one of those remarkable geniuses—like Aristotle—who made an impact on virtually every aspect of the intellectual life of his time. He was a scientist, a mathematician, a political reformer, and one of the early defenders of feminism. But he is best known for his ethical theories, particularly his defense of individual freedom (*On Liberty* [1859]) and his classic defense of utilitarianism (*Utilitarianism* [1863]). Mill amended Bentham's calculus of sheer *quantity* of pleasure with a conception of the *quality* of pleasure. Thus Mill insisted, "It is better to be a Socrates dissatisfied, than a pig satisfied."

The various forms of utilitarianism—all of them originating in the simple, appealing "principle of utility" formulated by Bentham and Mill—reflect a number of problems in the theory; each variation is an attempt to modify the theory to answer an objection. The first variation to the theory was Mill's objection to Bentham's purely quantitative theory, which placed too much emphasis on bodily pleasures and not enough on the harder-to-quantify pleasures of the mind and spirit—the arts, friendship, philosophy. A more recent variation in utilitarian theory is the formulation of rule utilitarianism—in contrast to act utilitarianism—as a way of meeting the objection that clearly wrong acts might, in a single instance, be shown to maximize pleasure and minimize pain for everyone involved. Rule utilitarianism blocks this possibility by insisting that a *class* of actions, not just a single instance, improves the general well-being.

Utilitarianism continues to be one of the most thoroughly discussed ethical theories and strategies of moral justification, but it is not without its continuing problems. As a theory of utility, it has always been accused of being "vulgar" and devoid of spiritual awareness. Indeed, Mill counters this objection even in *Utilitarianism,* when he answers religious critics who attack him for appealing morality to a businesslike calculation of pleasures instead of to God or the scriptures. Mill's reply is simply that God being good wants us to be happy, and so God Himself is a utilitarian and utilitarianism is just a precise way of interpreting God's will.

A more telling set of objections is aimed at the emphasis on *consequences* (whether of an action or a type of action) in utilitarian theory. When a moral principle is presented absolutely (as in the Ten Commandments, for example), it is accepted first, and the question of consequences does not arise—or arises only afterward. But when every action and every rule is subject to the test of consequences, a number of objections present themselves:

1. There usually isn't time to calculate all the consequences beforehand. (This objection does not apply to rule utilitarianism.)
2. We usually don't know enough to calculate all the consequences beforehand.
3. Very different kinds of consequences may be extremely difficult to compare. (Closing down the city art museum may save the taxpayers thousands of dollars, but what is the cultural "cost" of doing so?)
4. Couldn't the consequences of an act (or a class of actions) be positive and, nevertheless, the act be wrong? (Suppose it were demonstrated that adultery saves more marriages than it destroys and makes more people happy than miserable; would it then be the moral thing to do?)

Finally, the most dramatic objection to utilitarianism aims at the principle of utility itself. Mill protects the principle from abuse (for example, by a very powerful person who makes himself happy at everyone else's expense) by insisting that "everyone counts for one and only one." But even within this principle of equality, a serious ambiguity remains. Suppose a majority of the citizens of a town pass a tax law that, in effect, takes $500 from every member of the minority and, at the same time, cuts taxes by the same amount for every member of the majority (the balance coming from the education budget, no doubt). Leaving aside the difficulty of measuring amounts of pleasure and pain merely on the basis of dollar amounts (assume that everyone has about the same income and financial status), it seems clear that this act is defensible according to utilitarianism because it maximizes pleasure (makes more people happy). And yet, we would probably all agree, the act is clearly unjust. A second, more sadistic example favored by many critics of utilitarianism is this: Suppose that a rather sick society gets great joy out of the spectacle of a few innocent people being tortured to death. (Consider Rome during some of its darker days, for example.) On the utilitarian account, the great joy of the spectators—if it outweighs the suffering of the few victims—is sufficient to make their behavior moral. But this, we object, is surely unfair and immoral. What this seems to show is that utilitarianism cannot take proper account of justice. The well-being of the majority is one thing, but justice may be something else. Usually the two are commensurate, happily. Nevertheless, as an overall theory of the justification of morality, utilitarianism has been accused of failing a crucial test: it cannot provide adequate justification for some of our most important moral convictions.

Kant and Deontology

It is in reaction to the objections to utilitarianism, particularly its apparent inadequacy in accounting for justice, that a great many philosophers have turned to an older tradition in which moral principles are not conditional on consequences but are absolute. The origins of this theory go back to the beginnings of human history, when the word of the chief, or the king, or God, was given unconditionally and without invitation to appeal on the basis of consequences. Such theories are sometimes called *deontological* theories, from the Greek root *dein* meaning "to be obligated." In deontological theories, an act or a class of actions is justified by showing that it is right, not by showing that it has good consequences (although it is usually expected that both will be the case).

The foremost modern defender of a deontological theory is Immanuel Kant. He was reacting to the early "utility" theories of Hume and other "enlightenment" philosophers, and he anticipated the later objections to utilitarianism (Kant wrote 70 years before Mill) by insisting that what makes an act right or wrong cannot be its consequences—which are often entirely out of our hands and a matter of luck—but the principle (or "maxim") that guides the action. "Nothing . . . can be called good without qualification, except a *good will,*" he writes at the beginning of his *Grounding for the Metaphysics of Morals.* And having a good will means acting with the right intentions, according to the right maxims or principles, doing one's duty for its own sake rather than for personal gain. This is the heart of Kant's ethics, "duty for duty's sake," not for the sake of the consequences, whether one's own good or "the greatest good for the greatest number."

What is the court of appeal for deontological theories of justification? The utilitarian, like the "enlightened" egoist and the Aristotelian teleologist, could appeal to actual human desires and aspirations. But the deontological theory, as "unconditional" or "absolute," rejects just those desires and aspirations as the ultimate court of appeal (although for Kant and almost all deontologists, they nevertheless remain important). The answer must be, they appeal to *authority.* But this does not necessarily mean that the deontologist gives up moral responsibility and passes it on to God or those in power. Some deontologists, of course, do appeal morality to the authority of God. (Thus, the justification of morality by appeal to God's will has the earmarks of both a teleological and a deontological theory. It refers to purposes [God's purpose], but it is also an absolute appeal to His authority.) Other deontologists appeal to the law ("it doesn't matter what you think, it's the law"). But at least one leading deontologist believes that the appeal to authority necessary to justify morality is also an appeal to our own moral autonomy in deciding what is right and what is wrong. That deontologist is Kant, and his theory continues to be one of the two basic starting points of most modern ethical theories (the other being utilitarianism).

On Kant's theory, the court of appeal for the justification of morality is the court of reason, or what he calls "pure practical reason." Each of us is rational, which means that each of us has the ability to reason and arrive at the right way to act, by ourselves and without appeal to any "outside" authority. This capacity to reason and decide for ourselves is what Kant calls *autonomy* (opposed to *heteronomy,* being ruled by others). To justify morality, therefore, is to show that it is rational, and to justify any particular moral principle is to show that it is in accord with the principles of reason. Morality, we have already seen, is characterized by Kant as a system of categorical imperatives, that is, commands that are unqualified and unconditional. We can now appreciate better what this means; they are unqualified not only in the sense that they apply to everyone, without regard to their personal interests, but in the sense that they apply without regard to consequences of any kind. They are principles of reason and, as such, are not bound to the contingencies of life. (Here we can see a positive use of the gap between values and facts we spoke of; Kant takes this to be the heart of reason—that it envisions the world according to its own ideals and is not merely determined by the facts of the world.)

Because moral principles are rational principles, according to Kant, their justification must be a purely formal (or logical) justification. To prove that an act is immoral, it is not enough to show that its actual or probable consequences would be disastrous; we must demonstrate that its principle itself is "contradictory" and impossible. One of Kant's examples will serve as an illustration of what this means. Suppose I am considering borrowing money from you under false pretenses, by lying and telling you that I will pay you back next week (when in fact I will be in Hawaii, never to return). Now the utilitarian would ask for the consequences (whether of the act or of such an act); Kant asks for more. What if, he argues, I were to apply the "maxim" of my act (that is, the principle upon which I am acting) to everyone else, and urge them to act similarly? Since morality is essentially a product of reason, I must be able to do this, for I cannot apply principles to myself alone. (The utilitarian would agree with this.) What would be the result? It would be to undercut the whole practice of promising to repay borrowed money, and if anyone were to ask, Can I borrow some money and pay you back next week? everyone would simply laugh, for such words would have become meaningless. Thus, Kant points out, the maxim "contradicts" itself. It not only has disastrous consequences (the concern of the utilitarian), it undercuts its own meaning and betrays a purely formal inadequacy.

Deontological theories of justification seem to succeed where utilitarian theories fail—in the demonstration of the unconditional force of moral principles. But the deontologist runs into trouble, accordingly, just where the utilitarian (and teleologists in general) succeeds—in the concern for human happiness and well-being. The deontologist is not indifferent to such concerns—indeed, Kant in a curious passage even argues that we have a *duty* to be happy—but the emphasis on duty and rational, formal principles clearly relegates happiness to secondary consideration. For this reason, Mill accuses Kant of needing utilitarianism if he is to make sense of his deontological theory, and utilitarians ever since have felt, with some justification, that no theory of the good could possibly be acceptable unless it puts in first place the concern for happiness.

Social Contract Theory

We have seen that one of the recurrent problems in ethical theory is the problem of identifying the ultimate principles and values that support them. Should they be based on reason or the emotions? Is our ultimate moral goal happiness or ethical integrity of some other sort? Do we assess actions according to intentions or results? Is there some sort of ultimate authority that goes beyond human control (such as God), or are human beings the last stop in ethical reasoning? Furthermore, even if we can sort out these kinds of questions, we have seen that we are still subject to seemingly irreconcilable conflicts within a particular ethical system. Such problems sometimes threaten to overwhelm us, leaving us with the suspicion that there is no principled way to resolve them. One theory, represented in this volume by Thomas Hobbes and John Rawls, takes a practical approach to such problems through the idea of the social contract.

Social contract theory originated in political theory, but as we shall see, it offers a substantial moral theory as well. It begins with the question of what morality is for and answers it with a very simple claim: It is to enable us to live well together. Whether one takes it as a biological inevitability (as Aristotle does) or an historical accident, there is no denying that human beings live in society with one another. And it is equally undeniable that there are enormous benefits to communal living. Everything from potable water systems, to universities, to symphony orchestras is the result of cooperative living. The alternative to such arrangements is called the state of nature, in which each of us goes it alone, not only foregoing the sorts of benefits just mentioned, but living in competition with and in danger from other solitary souls. It makes sense, then, to join forces, and we do so by making an agreement, or contract, with others. We see, in other words, that we will benefit from working together rather than competing with one another. The social contract requires that we accept the rules of society, but in return we gain the benefits that such a society provides. By "signing" the social contract, we both secure our safety and enjoy the fruits of cooperative ventures.

However, there is a price to be paid for such advantages, namely the sacrifice of complete freedom. In order for social life to be possible, we must subject ourselves to rules that were absent from the state of nature. If I want to be sure you won't steal from me, I must agree that I will not steal from you. In other words, we make a contract whereby we both agree to forego certain liberties in order to gain others. For instance, we give up the liberty of taking whatever we like, but we gain the privilege of owning property securely. Likewise, we give up the freedom to drive at any speed we choose, but we gain the advantages of police protection. Like any contract freely entered into, however, the social contract is one that is, ideally, to our mutual benefit. That which we give up is less valuable than that which we gain.

There has been a good deal of discussion over whether this contract was in any historical sense actual, or only hypothetical, but that need not concern us here. For our purposes, the idea of the social contract enables us to account for and justify the rules under which we live. These rules can be legal and political (such as traffic regulations or electoral processes), but they can also be moral. What is morality on this account? It is the system of rules that is necessary for us to live in civil society. Thus, the injunction against lying is justified by the observation that the sorts of relationships and transactions that characterize social life would be impossible if lying was rampant. Why do we look down on cheating on tests? Because in order for the university to produce adequately qualified graduates, students must be fairly evaluated on the basis of merit rather than fraud. The general idea, then, is that we justify our moral rules in terms of what is required for us all to have as much freedom as possible, without violating the freedom of others.

The advantage of such a theory lies in its practicality. We need not make reference to any external authority (such as God) or to the "true nature" of human beings. All we need do is look at our social union and determine what rules are necessary in order to make it operate to everyone's advantage. Nevertheless, the social contract theorist faces problems. For instance, there may be disagreements about the value of the sacrifices and advantages involved, or which liberties should be given up in return for which advantages. (The national debate over handguns is an instance of this sort of problem: Those who are in favor of gun control are willing to forego the liberty of carrying a weapon in return for what they perceive as the benefit of having fewer guns in circulation, whereas those who are against such limitations consider the greater benefit to be the freedom to arm themselves.) There is the further problem of determining the scope of social and moral rules—how much should be a matter of an accepted morality, and how much should be left up to the individual? (Here, we might consider such contemporary controversies as those regarding smoking or euthanasia.) Although social contractarians have answers to such challenges (for instance, that moral rules should apply only to those activities that affect others), their claims do not necessarily escape controversy any more than other approaches.

Ethical Relativism

This introduction would not be complete without at least a mention of ethical relativism, although for obvious reasons, it will not be a doctrine that is explicitly propounded by any of our authors. (Friedrich Nietzsche is often accused of ethical relativisim, although in fact he warned against the dangers of this "decadent" way of thinking.) Ethical relativism begins with the observation that different cultures have radically different moral systems. Arranged marriages for very young girls are deemed right in some societies but disapproved of in ours. In some cultures, the appropriate thing for people to do when they have become too old to be productive is to die, whereas in ours, effort is often made to prolong life indefinitely. In some countries, women are excluded from political and commercial offices, while in others they are positively encouraged to enter them. And these are not simply matters of taste, the relativist points out. Rather, each society deems its practices to be morally *right*. Furthermore, and most importantly, the relativist claims that there is no way to adjudicate between the opposing claims—we have no basis for saying that one system is better than another. The relativist concludes that the identification of particular, disparate moral systems is as far as we can go in moral theory. In other words, the most we can say is that morality is relative to a particular society and culture. Within that culture, moral judgments are possible, but across cultures, we can do no more than point out the differences. Consequently, for the relativist ethics is no longer a prescriptive discipline, but one that is purely descriptive along the lines of sociology or anthropology.

What are we to say in response to such claims? If we want to counter ethical relativism, we might first point out that not *all* values are relative. Although different societies obviously have different sets of customs, there are some moral claims that we might assert to be universally valid. For instance, prohibitions against senseless torture of innocent children would seem to be morally wrong, regardless of one's culture. Although there are clearly culturally relative ways of raising children, ranging from forms of discipline to views toward marriage, the basic value of preventing unwarranted harm to children would seem to apply transculturally. The way we might then explain differences among societies would be in the way they interpret the basic value of protection of the innocent. Those cultures that advocate paternalistic protection of women might hold that arranging a marriage for a 13-year-old girl is the best way to further the value of protecting the young. On the other hand, if a culture such as ours believes women are just as capable of autonomy as men, arranging such a marriage will be viewed as a harm rather than a benefit. The idea behind this sort of response to relativism is the claim that there are universal values, but that they are often interpreted in different ways depending on the social norms prevalent in a society. If we understand ethics as an attempt to justify our moral principles, then the relativist has not necessarily shown that there are no further judgments we might make once we are confronted with the plurality of moral systems.

This leads to the second response many have made to the relativist's challenge, namely, that it leads to the impossibility of judging some systems to be better than others. If the relativist is right—if morality is completely determined by a particular society's beliefs—then it becomes impossible to judge one society as better or worse than another. In other words, if morality is relative, there is no overarching system by which to compare and evaluate different cultures. But if this is true, then we are unable to say that the genocide in Nazi Germany was wrong, at least from a morally independent, objective standpoint. If we embrace relativism, there is no such standpoint. The most we may be able to say is that Hitler's Germany had a different morality than our own; what we cannot say is that it was a worse one. For again, the relativist's argument entails that there is no further system beyond each particular culture's morality. As such, we can judge only within a specific society. Moreover, given the lack of ultimate principles, the relativist must rely on accepted and prevalent beliefs, or majority opinion. Although the example of Nazi Germany may be somewhat suspect insofar as there are complicated issues of who and how many accepted the Nazi regime, if we take morality to be nothing more than the set of principles by which a society guides itself, that of the Nazis will have constituted that culture's morality. To accept relativism, then, is to preclude many of the ethical judgments we often want to make. It should be noted, however, that ethical relativism is alive and well, and like other theorists, relativists have ways of answering the challenges posed against their theory.

Pluralism and History

One of the problems of a pluralist society is its inability to come to ready agreement on pressing moral issues (for example, the acceptability of nonstandard sexuality, the legitimacy of a "progressive" income tax). But this problem is in fact the other side of a virtue as well; it stimulates a degree of self-understanding that a less conflict-ridden society would not achieve, and it promotes the necessity of mutual understanding and tolerance that a nonpluralist would find unimaginable. This is emphatically not to say that we thereby learn to suspend ethical judgment or give up the aim of formulating a coherent and all-encompassing ethical system for ourselves. It is rather to say that articulation and argument, justification and mutual understanding are themselves among the most important virtues of our society, and by developing these abilities we simultaneously create and reinforce our own pluralistic society, however many differences and disagreements will always be found within it. Bertrand Russell often wrote that philosophy can teach us to ask better and better questions, even if it does not always provide us with answers. (And indeed, as we shall see in the readings from Russell, he never stopped challenging and reworking his own ethical views.)

It would be a mistake to see every philosopher from Plato to Sartre as engaged in a single enterprise and answering a single set of questions. They are participants in distinctive historical epochs and different cultures, and thus they express distinctive concerns and resolve different problems. It is perfectly acceptable to compare or contrast Aristotle and Kant on certain issues or to point out certain similarities between Saint Augustine and Sartre, but this must always be done with keen historical caution and the awareness that we are not just judging a dog show with slight variations among a few classic breeds. Ethics is a curious combination of self-awareness, history, self-criticism, and anthropology. It begins with a tradition that is as old as Western thought itself and ends, necessarily, in the question—OK, what do we do now?

Feminist Ethics

Several of the most urgent matters in contemporary ethical debate are raised by the strong (and growing stronger) voice of feminist ethics. Although some theorists offer substantive prescriptions, *feminist ethics* is primarily a critique of traditional theories of ethics and morality. Feminists begin with the observation that traditional Western accounts of ethics (at minimum) leave out a great deal. What is left out is often characterized as the experience of women (hence, the feminism with which it begins), but it can also be viewed as the realm of our private lives, and as such can include men as well as women. Perhaps the best way to clarify these claims is to examine a number of distinctions that have to do very generally with our moral experiences, including reason versus emotion, impartiality versus attachment, and pure justice versus caring. Feminist ethicists hold that traditional ethics deal with only one side of these dichotomies (the first in each pair), yet both sides are essential to a fully ethical life. Their criticism of traditional ethical theories runs the gamut from the accusation that such theories have a totally mistaken understanding of human nature, values, and morality in general, to the less extreme complaint that traditional theories are incomplete at best.

The first and perhaps most broad distinction is between the public and the private realms. Our public lives are characterized by the interactions that take place in the marketplace, the political arena, and in the sociopolitical and legal institutions that govern them. The private realm, on the other hand, represents those interactions in which personal relationships are key. As such it includes not only the home with its attendant commitments and obligations, but our friendships and other personal interactions as well. Now what we are asked to notice here is that very different ethical rules apply, and should apply, to the interactions that take place in these radically different parts of our lives. The public realm is governed by standards of fairness, impartiality, and reason, whereas in the private realm, the standards that make for moral behavior have more to do with caring, emotions, and partiality. Compare, for instance, the way you would treat a business competitor with the way in which you would approach your best friend. In the first situation it is both appropriate and desirable to seek your own interests within the rules of fair business transactions. Business transactions are often competitive and impersonal and are usually founded on the contract approach. This need not mean that they are unethical; it does mean that the rules of fair play are of a very different sort than those that apply to our personal relationships. In a friendship, we do not try to get the best of the other, nor do we treat our friends with impartiality. Rather, part of the essence of friendship is that special sense that this particular person matters a great deal to you.

The heart of the feminist ethics critique is the claim that traditional ethical theories apply only to the public realm and its attendant values, but this isn't, and shouldn't be, the whole of our moral lives. Consider some of the features we have pointed to in the approaches discussed so far. First and foremost is the emphasis on reason, often at the expense of the emotions, particularly affective love. We are asked to consider everyone equally and treat them accordingly. For instance, in the utilitarian approach we are instructed to maximize happiness, choosing the course of action that makes the most people happy, regardless of who those people are. As we pointed out, this may well involve the sacrifice of some people's interests, but the theory does not allow us to pick and choose among those affected for personal reasons.

Imagine a mother who faces the terrible choice between saving her own child and four other children whom she does not know. The universality requirement in utilitarianism would arguably demand that she save the four strangers over her own child. On this theory, this would be the *morally* right thing to do. But is this right? Do we really want to say that the woman who coldly calculates that four lives will be saved rather than one, even when the one is the child she gave birth to and has nurtured, is doing the *right* thing ethically speaking? Something seems to have gone wrong here. The problem is that reason cannot account for all aspects of our lives. Not only do we have particular attachments to some people rather than others, but this is desirable; it is an essential and enormous part of our value system. Not only *do* mothers love their children more than strangers, they *should* do so. The point is that reasoned impartiality and complete fairness lead to morally unacceptable results in certain moral situations.

Generally speaking, the public realm is governed by norms of justice, impartiality, rights, and reason. But the private realm is run according to very different rules: those of caring, of particularity, of contextuality, and of emotion. What has gone wrong with traditional ethical theories is that they take into account only one-half of our lives. At the same time, however, they purport to offer an account of the whole of morality. As a result, feminist ethicists (and other critics of standard approaches to ethics) point out that such theories must either hold that the private realm rules are wrong in some way (and that the mother should save the strangers over her own child) or that such interactions are not genuinely ethical ones. But consider again the general definition of ethics offered at the outset: the study of values, rules, and justifications. Surely the desperate situation of the mother involves hugely important values, and we can obviously justify her choice of action. Thus, it seems impossible to characterize this interaction as amoral or nonethical. However, if we do admit of its ethical nature but then must rely solely on reason and impartiality, we are led to the conclusion that she has acted wrongly in saving her own child. And this claim will surely strike most people as wrong.

We have been focusing on an extreme case, but the critique of traditional ethics is not limited to such unusual and desperate scenarios. Rather the deeper claim is that much of our lives is made up of interpersonal interactions, the character of which cannot be solely captured by standards of justice, reason, and impartiality. Our public and business lives are important, but no more so than our private lives with friends and family. To hold that all of morality can be subsumed under the former is not only incomplete, but it denigrates those intrinsically important parts of our lives in which emotional attachments and particular acts of caring are paramount.

There have been a variety of attempts to correct this imbalance, the most important perhaps, being a theory called "the ethics of care," developed by Carol Gilligan, Nel Noddings, and others. It is impossible to give a brief summary of this approach because it is as multifaceted as it is innovative. Indeed, one of the criticisms feminist ethicists offer against traditional ethics concerns the latter's assumption that there is such a thing as universal, right reason and that this is the basis for all moral action. As a result, feminist ethicists face the problem of asserting a new way to think about morality, while suggesting that there may be no single right way to think about it. One promising solution to this problem is offered by Virginia Held, who suggests that we need "a division of moral labor," one in which different moral theories apply to the radically different sorts of interactions we have. In general, however, feminist approaches to ethical theory seek to vindicate those moral experiences that do not fit neatly into the reason-based model of traditional theories. In so doing, they rectify what is surely a serious error, namely, the implication that action based on emotions, caring, and attachment to particular persons is less than fully ethical.

Because this is a text on classical sources in ethical theory and the area of feminist ethics is relatively new, we do not include a representative essay on feminist ethical theory. It is, however, an important example of the ongoing work in ethics, and an important response to the theories presented here.

Prologue

ETHICS AND RELIGION

Before philosophy, religion embodied the varied wisdom of the ages with regard to morals, ethics, and the good life. Judaism goes back almost three millennia, Christianity almost two. Islam is comparatively recent, dating back only a millennium and a half. In Asia, Hinduism goes back more than three millennia, Buddhism, Confucianism, and Taoism two and a half. All of these religions are now world religions, and their ethical prescriptions still define much of ethics.

THE HEBREW BIBLE

Tracing itself back to the third millennium B.C.E. to the patriarch Abraham, Judaism has provided a rich source of philosophy and philosophical disputation, first in the self-conception of the Hebrew people and their law, later in the teachings of the prophets (ninth-eighth century B.C.E.) and the extensive writings that became the Talmud, the body of law and commentaries based on the Torah. (The word "Jewish" comes from the name of the Kingdom of Judah, which after the death of Solomon comprised two of the twelve tribes of Israel.) Philosophical argument became so basic to the life of the ancient Hebrews that there was no need to distinguish it as a separate intellectual enterprise, "philosophy." Because of their commitment to the law, the Hebrews were perpetually interested in questions about the meaning of the law and how it instructed people to live and in questions about justice and the good society. Above all, the Hebrews were vitally interested in how they were to please their all-powerful, not always predictable God. Hebrew philosophy, accordingly, was primarily concerned with the nature of this God and the significance of the laws he had given to his people. The law would become central to Hebrew and later Jewish religious thinking in a way that it had not to any other people.

Ancient Hebrew philosophy was largely defined by these three key concepts: the belief in a single God, the sense of being favored or "chosen" by that God, and the importance of the law, given by God. The second, perhaps, might be dismissed as overly chauvinistic and too ethnically exclusive for philosophy, but the first and third concepts define not only the philosophy of the ancient Hebrews but provide the framework for virtually the entire course of Western history and philosophy, the One God and His Law.

Philosophically, the idea of a single, all-powerful God implied universality, a single set of rules and beliefs that would apply not only in this or that region or city-state, but everywhere, and to everyone. It is not entirely clear when the ancient Hebrews adopted the belief in one God, but it clearly followed a period during which they, too, acknowledged a plurality of competing gods and goddesses, one of whom became their favorite and who, in return, made them His "chosen people."

This compromise between monotheism and polytheism anticipated a number of complex problems that would prompt a good deal of Jewish, Christian, and Islamic theology. One enduring philosophical problem had to do with the relationship of the one God to Creation. Did God create a world that was independent of himself, or is He present in the world? How and why did He create the universe, and why did He do it as He did it? Why, in particular, did He create people "in his image," as the English translation of the Hebrew Bible puts it, and what is his continuing relationship with them?

Although Judaism emphasizes the dignity of the individual, it began, we should remember, as a tribal religion. The individual has meaning and dignity, first of all, insofar as he or she is a member of the community. But as in so many ancient societies, the formation of community is not left to chance. Judaism considers its status as "the Chosen People" to mean chosen by virtue of God's promise to their ancestor Abraham. Abraham was promised by God that his descendants would become a great nation. There is, accordingly, an exclusive, even racial element to Judaism, which would be firmly rejected by the early Christians, especially by Saint Paul. Jewishness is not so much a philosophy or a set of beliefs, according to this ancient viewpoint, as it is a matter of membership. Consequently, Jewish philosophy is not nearly as focused on the intricacies of theology and belief as on the meaning of membership in the Jewish community and the implications of that membership.

There is little by way of theology in the Old Testament, but the personality of God, if we may call it that, is rendered as clearly as if in a novel. The God of the Hebrews is, by His own admission, a jealous God. He is sometimes an angry God, a wrathful God. Any number of familiar stories from the old testament could be used to illustrate the point, but the large philosophical thesis—which one might compare with the early Greek view of Fate—is that the Hebrews' all-powerful, protecting God was extremely unpredictable, tempestuous, even whimsical. He could be easily enraged, and the disasters that befell the Hebrews were proof of this. On the one hand, the Hebrews were protected by their mighty God. On the other hand, this protection was by no means wholly reliable, and the lapses in God's protection had to be explained. The same problem arose concerning God's **"grace."** In Judaism as in much of Christianity, grace was bestowed by God as a matter of pure choice on His part. No one and no people were "entitled" to it.

The philosophy of the Hebrews must be understood in terms of this great anxiety regarding the Hebrew "covenant" with God. The covenant gave them some assurance, but when disaster struck—as it so often did, the Jews did not doubt their belief in God but rather *blamed themselves.* The prophets would speak almost with pride of the forces amassed against Israel, not as proof of God's abandonment but rather as proof of His displeasure with the Jewish people. The alternative interpretation, that they were being abandoned by God, was unthinkable to the Hebrews. Guilt was far preferable to the loss of one's faith, and it might be said that the Hebrews gave guilt its philosophical form. But in so doing, they also pushed human self-examination to depths it had never known before.

THE TEN COMMANDMENTS

[Exodus 20:1–17]

20 Then God spoke all these words:
2 I am the LORD your God, who brought you out of the land of Egypt, out
of the house of slavery; 3 you shall have no other gods before me.
4 You shall not make for yourself an idol, whether in the form of anything that is in heaven above, or that is on the earth beneath, or that is in the water under the earth.
5 You shall not bow down to them or worship them; for I the LORD your God am a jealous God, punishing children for the iniquity of parents, to the third and the fourth generation of those who reject me,
6 but showing steadfast love to the thousandth generation of those who love me and keep my commandments.
7 You shall not make wrongful use of the name of the LORD your God, for the LORD will not acquit anyone who misuses his name.
8 Remember the sabbath day, and keep it holy.
9 Six days you shall labor and do all your work.
10 But the seventh day is a sabbath to the LORD your God; you shall not do any work—you, your son or your daughter, your male or female slave, your livestock, or the alien resident in your towns.
11 For in six days the LORD made heaven and earth, the sea, and all that is in them, but rested the seventh day; therefore the LORD blessed the sabbath day and consecrated it.
12 Honor your father and your mother, so that your days may be long in the land that the LORD your God is giving you.
13 You shall not murder.
14 You shall not commit adultery.
15 You shall not steal.
16 You shall not bear false witness against your neighbor.
17 You shall not covet your neighbor's house; you shall not covet your neighbor's wife, or male or female slave, or ox, or donkey, or anything that belongs to your neighbor.

At Genesis 17 God makes a covenant with Abram, instructing him to change his name to Abraham and promising Abraham that he shall be "the ancestor of a multitude of nations." Abraham, who is childless, expresses skepticism that his 90-year-old wife Sarah (formerly, Sarai) can bear a child (with the sort of delightful audacity before God that one sees often in the Hebrew Bible, Abraham falls on his face and laughs). But God insists that Sarah will bear him a son in one year, and that his name will be Isaac.

[Genesis 17:1–22]

17 When Abram was ninety-nine years old, the LORD appeared to Abram, and
said to him, "I am God Almighty; walk before me and be blameless. 2 And I will
make my covenant between me and you and will make you exceedingly numerous." 3 Then Abram fell on his face; and God said to him, 4 "As for me, this
is my covenant with you: You shall be the ancestor of a multitude of nations.
5 No longer shall your name be Abram, but your name shall be Abraham; for I
have made you the ancestor of a multitude of nations. 6 I will make you exceedingly fruitful; and I will make nations of you and kings shall come from you. 7 I
will establish my covenant between me and you, and your offspring after you
throughout their generations, for an everlasting covenant, to be God to you and
to your offspring after you. 8 And I will give to you, and to your offspring after
you, the land where you are now an alien, all the laud of Canaan, for a perpet-
ual holding; and I will be their God."

9 God said to Abraham, "As for you, you shall keep my covenant, you and
your offspring after you throughout their generations. 10 This is my covenant,
which you shall keep, between me and you and your offspring after you: Every
male among you shall be circumcised. 11 You shall circumcise the flesh of your
foreskins, and it shall be a sign of the covenant between me and you.
12 Throughout your generations every male among you shall be circumcised
when he is eight days old, including the slave born in your house and the one
bought with your money from any foreigner who is not of your offspring.
13 Both the slave born in your house and the one bought with your money must
be circumcised. So shall my covenant be in your flesh an everlasting covenant.
14 Any uncircumcised male who is not circumcised in the flesh of his foreskin
shall be cut off from his people; he has broken my covenant."

15 God said to Abraham, "As for Sarai your wife, you shall not call her
Sarai, but Sarah shall be her name. 16 I will bless her, and moreover I will give
you a son by her. I will bless her, and she shall give rise to nations; kings of peoples shall come from her." 17 Then Abraham fell on his face and laughed, and
said to himself, "Can a child be born to a man who is a hundred years old? Can
Sarah, who is ninety years old, bear a child?" 18 And Abraham said to God,
"O that Ishmael might live in your sight!" 19 God said, "No, but your wife Sarah
shall bear you a son, and you shall name him Isaac. I will establish my covenant
with him as an everlasting covenant for his offspring after him. 20 As for Ishmael, I have heard you; I will bless him and make him fruitful and exceedingly
numerous; he shall be the father of twelve princes, and I will make him a great
nation. 21 But my covenant I will establish with Isaac, whom Sarah shall bear to
you at this season next year." 22 And when he had finished talking with him,
God went up from Abraham.

Sarah does indeed bear a son named Isaac, as God had promised to Abraham. But then, in one of the most powerful and terrifying stories in the Hebrew Bible, God tests Abraham. God commands Abraham to bind his son Isaac and to offer him as a sacrifice to God on Mount Moriah. In a particularly poignant moment of the story Isaac asks Abraham, "Father . . . the fire and the wood are here, but where is the lamb for a burnt offering?" unaware that he himself is the lamb to be sacrificed. On the mountain Abraham binds his son and prepares to sacrifice him. But just as he is about to kill his son, God speaks to Abraham and stops him, "for now I know that you fear God, since you have not withheld your son, your only son, from me."

The apparent (some say, glaring) opposition between faith and ethics in this story has captured the imagination of many theologians and philosophers. Søren Kierkegaard, a Danish philosopher, argued that the story illustrates that religious faith must ultimately take precedence over ethics. If Abraham is willing to commit a terrible ethical crime in order to prove his faith to God, he can justify his action only if that faith is more important than his enormous ethical responsibility to his son. Moreover, Isaac represents to Abraham not only his son, but the promised future of Abraham's people. Isaac, remember, is the son in whom God's covenant with Abraham is to be fulfilled. So by his willingness to sacrifice Isaac, Abraham shows that his own personal faith in God is more important than his son, the divinely given ethical prohibition against murder, and even the entire future of Abraham's people. This story is still more disturbing when we consider other divinely justified "suspensions of the ethical" (the expression is Kierkegaard's). What about an insane person who justifies the murder of his or her children on the basis that "God instructed it"? Or a terrorist who explodes him or herself and others on the basis of a (sincere) misinterpretation of divine will? How should we distinguish Abraham's journey to Mount Moriah from other, seemingly similar, justifications for murder?

[Genesis 22:1–19]

22 After these things God tested Abraham. He said to him, "Abraham!" And he
said, "Here I am." 2 He said, "Take your son, your only son Isaac, whom you
love, and go to the land of Moriah, and offer him there as a burnt offering on one
of the mountains that I shall show you." 3 So Abraham rose early in the morning,
saddled his donkey, and took two of his young men with him, and his son Isaac;
he cut the wood for the burnt offering, and set out and went to the place in the distance that God had shown him. 4 On the third day Abraham looked up and saw
the place far away. 5 Then Abraham said to his young men, "Stay here with the
donkey; the boy and I will go over there; we will worship, and then we will come
back to you." 6 Abraham took the wood of the burnt offering and laid it on his son
Isaac, and he himself carried the fire and the knife. So the two of them walked on
together. 7 Isaac said to his father Abraham, "Father!" And he said, "Here I am,
my son." He said, "The fire and the wood are here, but where is the lamb for a
burnt offering?" 8 Abraham said, "God himself will provide the lamb for a burnt
offering, my son." So the two of them walked on together.

9 When they came to the place that God had shown him, Abraham built an
altar there and laid the wood in order. He bound his son Isaac, and laid him on
the altar, on top of the wood. 10 Then Abraham reached out his hand and took the

knife to kill his son. [11] But the angel of the LORD called to him from heaven, and
said, "Abraham, Abraham!" And he said, "Here I am." [12] He said, "Do not lay
your hand on the boy or do anything to him; for now I know that you fear God,
since you have not withheld your son, your only son, from me." [13] And Abraham looked up and saw a ram, caught in a thicket by its horns. Abraham went
and took the ram and offered it up as a burnt offering instead of his son. [14] So
Abraham called that place "The LORD will provide"; as it is said to this day. "On
the mount of the LORD it shall be provided."

15 The angel of the LORD called to Abraham a second time from heaven,
[16] and said, "By myself I have sworn, says the LORD: Because you have done
this, and have not withheld your son, your only son, [17] I will indeed bless you,
and I will make your offspring as numerous as the stars of heaven and as the
sand that is on the seashore. And your offspring shall possess the gate of their
enemies, [18] and by your offspring shall all the nations of the earth gain blessing
for themselves, because you have obeyed my voice." [19] So Abraham returned to
his young men, and they arose and went together to Beer-sheba; and Abraham
lived at Beer-sheba.

THE NEW TESTAMENT

Although Christianity is founded on the life and recorded teachings of Jesus (5 B.C.E.–A.D. 29 or 30), the Christian church properly begins with Jesus' crucifixion and the subsequent conviction of his disciples that he was raised by God from the dead. It is then that the divinity of Jesus is proclaimed—the one in whom "the Word became flesh." And it is then that Jesus is declared by his disciples to be the prophesied Messiah (*Christos*), with the authority to make God's mind known to man, to reveal the true meaning of God's law, to perform miracles of healing and transformation, to forgive sins, and most importantly, to assume full responsibility for the eternal destiny and welfare of mankind. Although the law was the crucial ethical and religious concept for the Hebrew tradition, the divine power of forgiveness of Jesus Christ would become the central ethical and religious concept for the Christian tradition.

Christian philosophy, as it is expressed in the four Gospels, the Acts, and the many letters of the "New Covenant" or New Testament, depends largely on four beliefs:

1. The belief in the divine creation of the universe (a belief that comes from, and is shared with, Judaism).
2. The belief that there is an afterlife (a belief shared with Judaism and most other religions), which includes a heaven to reward those who are redeemed from sin and a hell for those who are not redeemed.
3. The belief that, although Jesus was a man like other men, subject to hunger, pain, sorrow, and even ignorance, he was also the divine Son of God.
4. The belief that all human beings are damned as sinners by original sin, and thus in need of redemption, and yet can be redeemed by accepting the free forgiveness offered by God through his son, Jesus Christ.

A fifth belief, also central to Christian philosophy but emerging slowly as the Christian church grows, is the doctrine of the Trinity, or the three-sided nature of God. According to this doctrine, God, although undivided and essentially one, nonetheless expresses his nature in three ways: as the Father, or divine, transcendent and eternal moral creator (witnessed to by the prophetic tradition in the Hebrew Bible); as the Son, who appeared on earth and in time as a human being; and as the Holy Spirit, which works through the Christian church and its members to guide them on earth. As one might suppose, this Trinitarian creed has been the subject of heated debate and the source of much "heresy" throughout the history of Christianity, and although it poses an interesting metaphysical problem (can one thing be both single and plural), it is not central to the ethics of the Christian church.

Beginning with the Hebrew ideas of a single, all-powerful God and the importance of a moral life as described by the God-given law, the New Testament introduces a fundamental ethical concept that is not emphasized in the Hebrew Bible: forgiveness. It is insisted that, after the fall from grace and expulsion from paradise, all humans are sinners, and will suffer moral failure because of their sinful state. Although this claim is a bit depressing, it makes an important philosophical (and psychological) point: in fact people do tend to make moral mistakes very frequently. For the Christian, this tendency to sin is a consequence of our nature as depraved beings, isolated from God by original sin, but it is importantly also a consequence of our free will: we are responsible for the sinful choices we make. But the "Good News" (gospel) is that we are not damned as sinners. The human appearance of Christ is God's new covenant with his people: if we accept Christ as our Savior, God will forgive our sins and grant us entrance into heaven when we die. That forgiveness is often, but not always, tied to Christ's death on the cross. For example, Martin Luther, the sixteenth-century reformer of the church, argued that Christ's crucifixion was the atonement for the original fall of mankind, and it was only through Christ's suffering the punishment that humankind was due that forgiveness of the human race was possible. More recent arguments have proposed, however, that Christ's crucifixion is only a sign to remind us of the need for divine forgiveness, and that the sacrifice of Christ was not in fact necessary for God's forgiveness.

Because of the emphasis on forgiveness in the New Testament, philosophers and theologians have worried about the role of damnation and hell in Christianity. For some philosophers (for example, the early Christian philosopher Augustine), human beings are predestined either to heaven or hell, and hell constitutes eternal damnation. But some thinkers believe that eternal damnation is inconsistent with the Christian doctrine of forgiveness and argue that hell is a temporary, purgatorial condition, which will eventually result in salvation. If hell is eternal suffering without any morally good result, how can this be reconciled with the divine goodness and sovereignty of God? Or perhaps hell is simply annihilation, and the consciousness of the damned ceases to exist (therefore not suffering, but being excluded from the bliss of eternal salvation)?

The philosopher Nietzsche once wrote that, "were it not for Paul, the world would never have heard of a minor Jewish sect whose master died on the cross." This is too strong, of course, and a Christian will reasonably reply: "But were it not for Paul, God would have chosen someone else to spread the gospel." But Nietzsche's point is an important one: much of what we now understand as Christian doctrine, and especially Christian ethics, is developed in the letters of the apostle

Paul (A.D. 10–64–67). Paul (whose name at the time was Saul) was a Greek Jew and a Roman citizen who had been an officially sanctioned persecutor of Christians and the early Christian church. But in a famous (and perhaps legendary) donkey ride outside of Damascus, he had a vision that converted him to Christianity (Paul was susceptible to visions and ecstasies throughout his life and may well have been an epileptic). He changed his name to Paul and became perhaps the most zealous—and certainly the most influential—Christian the world has yet seen. He traveled through Arabia, to Jerusalem, and then later to Macedonia, Athens, Syria and Rome, making his way mostly on foot and establishing and reforming churches as he went. His thought is preserved for us in his letters, or epistles, to the members of the various churches he helped to establish or reform (at least 9 of the 13 epistles attributed to Paul are regarded as genuine).

Paul's letters are full of practical advice, both moral and otherwise, to the churches, on subjects as diverse as the occasional early Christian practice of offering meat to idols (he was opposed to it) and the kind treatment of slaves (he was in favor of it). He importantly emphasizes the imminent return of Christ to earth, which will result in the end of human history and the judgement of all mankind. This creates both a hope for the young Christian church (they, the righteous, will be rewarded, but the Romans who persecute them and all the other unrighteous will be harshly punished) and an urgency to practice the Christian life. He always stresses the importance of community to the life of the Christian and repeatedly reminds his readers of the primacy of the family and family life (he frequently makes practical suggestions about how a good family should be run). But the two most important concepts for Paul are faith and love.

For Paul, righteousness or virtue before the law of God must be attained by faith, and not by "works" of moral worth. He argues (in "Romans" and elsewhere) that the crucial difference between Judaism and Christianity is that the Hebrew tradition believes that good works alone—the proper performance of the law—will grant salvation. But he writes that this belief is the "stumbling stone" of the Hebrew tradition, because the only way to escape damnation and guarantee salvation is through faith in God and in his son, Jesus Christ. Paul is never entirely clear on what "faith" is (the term is notoriously difficult to define), but he writes that "faith comes from what is heard, and what is heard comes through the word of Christ" (Romans 10:17), suggesting that sincere belief in the words and the life of Christ are the essential elements of faith.

Love—a term no easier to define than faith—is considered by Paul to be at the very center of Christ's teaching and also at the core of all the Hebrew Ten Commandments. He argues that the Ten Commandments may be summed up in the one of the two commandments Jesus offered to one of the scribes when he was disputing with the Sadducees (a Hebrew sect): "You shall love your neighbor as yourself." We should notice that this is much stronger stuff than the similar (and much easier) maxim: "Do unto others as you would have them do unto you." Truly loving another as you love yourself seems to presume an understanding of, and dedication to, the interests of other people that is difficult to imagine. Later Christian philosophers

All translations from *New Revised Standard Version Bible.* Oxford University Press, New York and Oxford, 1989.

such as Søren Kierkegaard will argue with Paul that the whole of Christian ethics is summed up by this one simple (but very difficult to follow) commandment.

Like the ancient Greek moralist Socrates, Jesus did not write down any of his teaching. This task was left to his disciples, and all of what is recorded of his life and teaching is in the four eponymous gospels written by his disciples Matthew, Mark, Luke, and John.

The duly famous "Sermon on the Mount" is the most complete single statement we have of Jesus' beliefs (although twentieth-century biblical scholarship has thrown some doubt on its authenticity). Here Jesus introduces many of his great ethical and religious themes: that the poor and the persecuted will be rewarded for their sufferings in the next life; that a good person must do good works and spread the words of Jesus; that Jesus comes "not to abolish, but to fulfill" the law and the words of the prophets; that we should not repay evil with evil, but should rather "turn the other cheek"; that we should "strive first for the kingdom of God" and worry about worldly matters second; that we should not judge others; that one should "do to others as you would have them do to you"; and, perhaps most important, that we should love our enemies rather than hate them.

[Matthew 5:1–48]

5 When Jesus saw the crowds, he went up the mountain; and after he sat down, his disciples came to him. 2 Then he began to speak, and taught them, saying:

3 "Blessed are the poor in spirit, for theirs is the kingdom of heaven.

4 "Blessed are those who mourn, for they will be comforted.

5 "Blessed are the meek, for they will inherit the earth.

6 "Blessed are those who hunger and thirst for righteousness, for they will be filled.

7 "Blessed are the merciful, for they will receive mercy.

8 "Blessed are the pure in heart, for they will see God.

9 "Blessed are the peacemakers, for they will be called children of God.

10 "Blessed are those who are persecuted for righteousness' sake, for theirs is the kingdom of heaven.

11 "Blessed are you when people revile you and persecute you and utter all kinds of evil against you falsely on my account. 12 Rejoice and be glad, for your reward is great in heaven, for in the same way they persecuted the prophets who were before you.

13 "You are the salt of the earth; but if salt has lost its taste, how can its saltiness be restored? It is no longer good for anything, but is thrown out and trampled under foot.

14 "You are the light of the world. A city built on a hill cannot he hid. 15 No one after lighting a lamp puts it under the bushel basket, but on the lampstand, and it gives light to all in the house. 16 In the same way, let your light shine before others, so that they may see your good works and give glory to your Father in heaven.

17 "Do not think that I have come to abolish the law or the prophets; I have come not to abolish but to fulfill. 18 For truly I tell you, until heaven and earth pass away, not one letter, not one stroke of a letter, will pass from the law until all is accomplished. 19 Therefore, whoever breaks one of the least of these commandments, and teaches others to do the same, will be called least in the